ME, YOU & 26.2

DEAR EMILY

I HOPE YOU FIND INSPIRATION & EXCITEMENT FROM MY FIRST-TIMER STORIES & MY STORIES AS YOU KEEP ON READING. SO GLAD YUB BROUGHT US TOGETHER.

ME, YOU & 26.2

Coach Denise's Guide to Get You to Your First Marathon—One Mile At A Time

DENISE SAURIOL

You must do the thing you think you cannot do.
—Eleanor Roosevelt

DEDICATION

To my sister, Debbie O'Connor, who inspired me to run my first marathon after she did it first - she made what I thought was super-human, human.

To my running coach, Greg Domantay, who believed in me until I believed in myself. – he taught me to never limit my own possibility.

To my therapist, Melissa Mondschain and to Bill W. who helped me finally realize that everything I was looking for was already inside of me.

CONTENTS

From 26.2 to Your Coach

My brother Mike and I at the start of the 2009 Chicago Marathon. This was months after surviving a devastating car accident.

One step. One step is all it took to re-set my life and my relationship with running. On August 16, 2009, I was running to Central Park to start the New York City Half-marathon. Needless to say, I never made it to the start line. Instead, I ended up on a stretcher in the emergency room of New York–Presbyterian Hospital. I started the morning like I always do before a race - with a quick warm-up run to the start line. On, my warm-up, I encountered an intersection with construction taking place. Scaffolding surrounded the construction area seemingly protecting pedestrians from harm but obstructing my view of the other three corners of the intersection. As I neared the crosswalk, I made a mental note of a hose lying in the middle of the crosswalk - all I needed was to trip and injure myself on my way to the race! I cautiously stepped over the hose and stepped forward to resume my warm-up run.

A car then came out of nowhere. The impact sent me flying. I flew onto the hood and shattered the windshield with my body weight. I then flew off the hood and landed in front of the car slamming my head against the pavement. In shock, I crawled to the sidewalk to get out of the way of getting run over. Everyone says that your life flashes before your eyes when you are faced with death. This was not my experience, rather, my thoughts were consumed with if I was going to die, get run over or become paralyzed. There were so many Thank God moments that day. The most important was that I could walk, talk and breathe on my own after such a traumatic injury. For this reason, I celebrate August 16th as my re-birthday. That day, Denise 2.0 was released to the world.

I broke vertebrae L1 through L5 but thankfully, I did not require any invasive surgery. My mom moved in with me as I needed assistance with daily living –dressing myself, lifting and transportation. It took me months before I felt safe in a car, let alone next to traffic. I wore a back brace for over two months and underwent intensive physical therapy to regain function. When my orthopedic doctor gave me medical clearance to start running again he encouragingly said that I would come back faster and better than ever. This didn't matter to me then and even now. My near-death experience taught me the importance of valuing each day and each experience. I am grateful that I CAN run, that I CAN race, that I CAN see the world more intimately through running it, that I CAN transform a shitty day to a good one just by going on a run, and that I CAN befriend strangers every day with runners speak. You see, now when I run, it's more about the journey than the destination.

There had to be a reason for my survival. I didn't recognize it at the time but my relationship with running leading up to my accident was very myopic. My life revolved around all things marathoning. Work, fun, vacations and relationships were built around my training and my races. I was logging 60 to 70 miles a week of running at the time. If I missed a workout, I would beat myself up. If I didn't set a new personal record (PR) at a race, I would beat myself up. Even when I did get a PR, I would be proud of myself for a brief moment but then focus on chasing the next PR.

My injury and subsequent lengthy recovery inspired my desire to give back to running for what it had given to me over the years. It gave me confidence. It gave me friendships. It showed me what else was possible in my life. My relationship with running came full circle. I was grade school Denise again, the young girl, who loved how running made her feel confident and free. Once Denise 2.0 started running again, I stopped using running to define me and instead used it to fuel me. That was when I decided to start coaching part-time. I founded my coaching business Run for Change with the motto, "Change within Change for Others." Personally, I knew how much running had changed me and my running friends, so I wanted to share running with anyone who came my way. My mission as a coach is to help people reach their goals whether it be walking their first mile or running their first 100-mile race – overcoming both physical and mental challenges.

On one end of the spectrum, I want to reintroduce running or even walking to those running naysayers out there who don't like running. Let them know that running is fun and that it is not like gym class unless you want it to be. Running as an adult, you get to set the pace, location and distance that you run. It is almost a guarantee too that you will feel better afterwards. On the opposite end of the spectrum, I want to encourage runners that are similar to Denise 1.0, to "run" a race every now and then and to not "race" every race. To know you are enough. Our race results, degrees, pounds on a scale, GPA, job titles, pant size, etc. are just extensions of us. They do not define us. Enjoy the journey. High five the kids you pass on a race course. Help someone in your circle run their first race. Take and give a FREE HUG to/from the spectators cheering us all on. There is also a group of runners in the middle of the spectrum that I want to inspire to not quit before they even try. To try to get faster, to qualify for Boston, to try an ultramarathon, try a triathlon, etc. So many times, in life and in running we quit before we even start. Not trying is the real failure. I want to be the one who believes in them until they believe it. Just like Coach Greg did for me.

In October 2015, I lost my cousin, Hikin' Dave Sauriol. He was 48 years old, a father of six and as passionate about hiking as I am about marathoning. When David passed unexpectedly, it was the first time in my life that I realized that today is not a guarantee. I always knew that tomorrow was not guaranteed. That moment on, I have had a virtual hour glass in front of my face reminding me that I do not get a "do over" card. It is not enough to be aware of this reality. I also need to live by it. That is why one of my guiding principles is to minimize any residue of regret and maximize failing forward. I knew in my core that if I didn't follow my heart and become a full-time running coach, I would regret it. It didn't matter what anyone else thought about this decision. What mattered is what my heart was telling me. Helping someone do something they didn't think they could do fuels my soul. Not to mention, I have always believed that the more people you meet in life, the richer your life becomes. A full soul and a rich life are my new definition of success.

Coach Denise – Marathon Whisperer

Meet First-Timer, Frank H.

One word to describe my first marathon:
Awesome

Before training for the marathon, I'd always run too hard, too fast and would end up getting injured. Those shin splints and blisters kept me from running all that often. However, a body like this doesn't happen by accident! In signing up for a marathon, I wanted to both challenge myself and get healthier and this seemed like a good way to do both. It wasn't so much as an individual or outside influence that inspired me to sign up for a marathon, as it was a big challenge that would require consistent, focused discipline from within. I didn't really think about any other marathons when I signed up for my first. The goal of running my first 26.2 was ominous enough. I didn't need to make it any more daunting. Now that I have run one, Coach Denise keeps asking me if I would run another. Never say never, coach!

Through training for the marathon, I learned that running can be both awesome and shitty. I love seeing the sun rise over Lake Michigan as I work hard to improve my physical fitness. After my runs, I feel amazing and like I'm ready to bite the ass off a bear. However, I dreaded the next run. I don't know why, given how amazing I felt afterwards.

I found that my ability to accomplish goals is directly related to what I think I'm capable of. In other words, if you think you can complete a marathon, you're right. If you think you can't complete a marathon, you're right. So, at the end of the day, it's your ability to control your thoughts that controls your ability to complete a marathon, or any other goal, for that matter.

One thing that really surprised me on race day was what a massive event it is. I had no idea how many volunteers, spectators, medical staff, police and barricades it takes to make it happen. The energy and motivation of the crowd is amazing. In training, I didn't experience much, if any, crowd support as most of my runs were solo or one on one with Denise. The crowd on race day was a huge, positive boost.

Mile 1: My First 26.2

That's me at my first marathon, Chicago 1994!

I first discovered running in the 4th grade and we have been best friends ever since. I tried making friends with basketball and volleyball but we just couldn't click. I owe this to my lack of eye-hand-ball coordination. You can't say I didn't try. Running on the other hand was the only sport that was natural for me. I just had to put my shoes on and move forward. Though our friendship initiated from happenstance, I never expected to thrive so much from the mental, social and emotional benefits of running. Running has always made me feel better. When I am chewing on a problem, it's amazing how going for a run, helps me find clarity and direction to tackle that problem. It has enriched my life with so many friendships that I otherwise would have missed out on. Running becomes the common language that brings strangers together. It is the gift that keeps giving.

I tried out for basketball and volleyball in high school but didn't make either team. Our cross-country team though, didn't require try outs. You just had to show up and you were on the team. This is similar to running clubs around the world. There are no tryouts, you just show up and you are part of the club. Your age and pace take a back seat. At our cross-country meets, only the times from each school's top 7 runners counted in deciding who won the meet. The rest of the runner's finish times didn't count. Before each meet, our coach would rattle off the finish times he wanted from each of the top 7 girls. Throughout my 3 years on the team, my friend Cheryl and I would never hear our names called. We nicknamed ourselves miscellaneous and etcetera! Before our meets, I would tell Cheryl, "Miscellaneous, I want you to run "x"" and she would tell me, "Etcetera, I want you to run "y"." Ask anyone that was fast in high school and it's a guarantee that they still know their times. I have no idea what my times were, let alone the distances that I ran. The statistics of running were again secondary to me. What I valued in running was how empowered it made me feel, how it helped me deal with my anxiety and the friends it introduced me to. I continued to run throughout college and in to my early adulthood. Running became as innate as brushing my teeth and my daily dose of therapy.

I never thought, let alone imagined running a marathon because I thought the marathon was only for fast people, for people that went to college on a running scholarship, for people in the "top 7" or for all of those kids that ran faster than me in gym class. Boy, was I wrong. My older sister, Debbie proved my theory wrong when she ran her first marathon in the fall of 1993. At the time, Debbie and I were running five to six days a week. We would run however many miles we felt each day just for the fun of it. Our paces and finish times were secondary to how running made us feel. Heck, we didn't even own a running watch and only knew our pace when we would get our race results mailed to us. Each summer, we would run a couple of 5Ks and 10Ks. In the fall, we then would run a half-marathon. On marathon Sunday back in the fall of 1993, Debbie came home with her Chicago marathon medal and finisher shirt. I was inspired, intrigued and in awe! Internally, I thought, "What the piss, if she can do it, I can do it!"

Fast forward to October 30, 1994. That day, SCITED and all, I toed the line for my first marathon. Just like most first-timers, I was going to be a "one and done" marathoner. Heck, I didn't even know for sure if I was going to be a "one" marathoner. I did not know what I was getting into or if I would finish but I knew I was going to give it my all. After all, if my sister and running mate, Debbie could do it, I could do it too! Once the gun went off marathon morning, I was no longer SCITED. I was EXCITED in an uppercase, bold, 45-point font kind of way! I settled in behind a woman who was running slightly in front of me. About 8 miles in, I noticed that she was veering to the right of the course almost up on to the sidewalk. I didn't understand why she ran that way until, out of the blue, it was O P R A H! Yes, Oprah was out on the course high-fiving and cheering on the runners. Weeks earlier, she had just run her first marathon at the Marine Corps Marathon. Yes, Oprah was a first-timer just like you! I gleefully high-fived Oprah and then got back to business. Between the energy of the crowd and just high-fiving THEE Oprah, I had that runners high and more! I thought, "This is awesome, I love this!" Fast forward to mile 21 when I hit the proverbial wall and my thoughts quickly changed to "Where is Oprah?" and "This hurts so bad that I am N.E.V.E.R. doing this again."

That voice in my head at mile 21 was wrong. Once it sunk in that the impossible is now my reality, the thought of "one and done-ing" got replaced with "that wasn't so bad" and "I want to do that again but faster!" This happens to about 90% of us after we become a marathoner. I still don't have the right words to describe the igniting transformation that was triggered that day. I just know that prior to crossing that finish line, I was the girl who struggled feeling "X" enough. That day, I found the confidence that I had always been searching for.

I ran a couple more marathons on my own and was able to bring my finish time down. Seeing my time drop made me want to stretch myself again with the goal of qualifying for the Boston Marathon. Yes, the girl who didn't think she could run one marathon now had her eye on the holy grail of marathoning: Boston. As out of reach to me that first marathon was, so was qualifying for Boston. Which is exactly why I wanted to aim for it.

In 1999, I met a girl who had qualified for Boston on her first marathon. Holy speedster! I asked her how she did it and she said she ran track workouts. She invited me to her coach's track workouts. I immediately replied, 'No way, that is like high school gym class!" "Running fast hurts!" About a month later, I finally caved and started attending Coach Greg Domantay's marathon training. This was another level of running. The workouts hurt, but I saw the results on my watch. Not to mention, after surviving one of his workouts, I felt invincible because I had to call on extra grit to get through them. Being around my coach and the other runners inspired and pushed me more than I would have pushed myself running alone.

Coach Greg found untapped talent in me that I did not even know existed. The first season with him, I got my Boston qualifier! I ran a 3:37! The confidence that I gained from my first marathon magnified when I qualified for THEE Boston! At that point, my training and racing became the first thing in my life that one, I was good at and two, if I worked hard, I knew I would see the results. In the eight years working with Greg, I brought my marathon time down from 4:28 to 3:15. In 2008, I even won a $1,000 prize from the Chicago marathon for being the fastest Illinois Masters Female. Not bad for a former "back of the packer."

This was about the time my training and racing became myopic. As mentioned earlier, I was using my running to define me (among other things). I am not discounting the accomplishments that I have achieved in and out of running, as they showed my resilience, drive and grit. My problem was that I was putting more value on these external accomplishments than I was on myself. Gratefully, my car accident rerouted me back to the healthy relationship I had when running first found me.

Never in a million miles could I have imagined that my best friend from 4th grade would lead me to a career I love.

Meet First-Timer, Lily G.

One word to describe my first marathon: Incredible

I was never very athletic as a kid. I did a lot of extracurricular activities, but never any sports! I hated gym class! I didn't really get into running until I was a freshman in college. I was training to be an opera singer, and a lot of that involves getting rejected by people who don't think you're right for the part they're casting. I needed an activity that made me feel better about myself and that wasn't about competing with anyone except myself. Around the same time, my flute teacher had been diagnosed with breast cancer, so I joined a team to raise money for her at a local 5K. After that, I was hooked on running because it was an activity that boosted my self-esteem and also gave back to the community.

Through training for a marathon, I learned that I am mentally tough. Even though my body is not your typical "runner's body," it's your mental toughness that is even more important than being able to move quickly through the course. Running has always been the thing that reminds me that I am a strong person. It makes me feel good about myself and reminds me that I am so much more than a failed audition or a bad review in the newspaper. Competition is what I do every day as an opera singer. I go into a room and try to convince someone to hire me for one role that 500 people want. When I lace up my shoes, it is just me and the pavement. I tally those miles alone and I stand at the finish line alone, because I am only competing against myself.

Anyone can run a marathon. I really promise you this. It is a mind game more than anything else. You will get used to having sore legs. You will get used to the chafing. The part that is most important is believing that you can do it. You must resign yourself to the idea that you will make it to the finish line. Don't let the self-doubt win! As coach Denise would tell us, if you do your homework there is no reason you won't make it to the end. Unless of course, you tell yourself that you can't. Believe you can!

One thing that I learned on race day was that running really is a treat to myself, and not a tithing to the god of misery for my transgressions. During the marathon, I SMILED the whole time! The crowd's energy was infectious and I was so happy to be part of the festivities. The next time I train for a marathon, I will try to smile more!

Mile 2: YOU Too Can Do 26.2

That's me, your coach!
Chapter focus: Giving you the OOMPH to sign up for
Marathoning 101

Don't think you can do a marathon? Remember, I didn't think I could do one until my sister did it. All you have to do is watch a marathon live and in person and you will see every age, size and pace out there 26.2-ing. It's raw, human grit and will power at its finest. Better yet, volunteer at a marathon near you for a little dose of human inspiration. Think 26.2 miles is even too far to drive? I used to think that too, until I ran my first marathon. Part of the fear factor of this distance is that a lot of people fast forward from 0 to 26.2 miles right out of the gate. They think of where they are at in the moment with running or not running for that matter. They then get rightfully overwhelmed advancing to 26.2. Instead, you get 20+ weeks to prepare for that milestone.

I want you to think of training for the marathon as enrolling in a class. You will get a syllabus (training plan). You will do your homework (training runs). You can study alone or with your cohort (solo runs or group runs). You can get a tutor (coach). Lastly, you will take your final exam (the marathon). You wouldn't take a class in Mandarin and then have the final a week later, right? Same with Marathoning 101. You have a whole semester to get to 26.2 miles. You will see that each training run you complete will give you the physical and mental endurance to close the deal on this distance. With this class, whether you get an A or a D grade, you pass! Instead of getting a report card in the mail though, you get a medal, a finisher's shirt and an indescribable feeling that will ignite your soul! Training for a marathon or any race for that matter is very methodical. You just add heart! The key requirement with this class though, is that it has be an elective. You have to *want* it. It can't be a class you *have* to take. That *want* is what is going to drive you to do your homework. That *want* is what you will call on in the latter part of the marathon when the going gets tough.

Still not convinced that you have a marathon in you? Sometimes it takes someone else believing in you until you believe it. Let me be that someone! That is what my coach did for me and what I do for my clients. Think about the last time you did something that you initially thought was out of reach. You were probably overly excited about the new adventure into the path unknown but at the same time overly scared about the path into the unknown. I call this feeling SCITED (scared and excited). I believe that the SCARED component keeps us hungry, humble and also shows that we respect the endeavor. The EXCITED component gives us the courage to make that parachute-less jump. SCITED moments are when we are truly showing up in our life and also the moments that reset our status quo, baby!

As I mentioned earlier, when my sister, Debbie ran her first marathon, she made a feat that I thought was Super-Human, Human. My friend Holly did the same thing for me when she completed her first Ironman triathlon. My friend Corey inspired me to start my own software consulting business when he did it first. Side note about Corey: he is signed up for his first marathon as I type this! Can you say the "Inspiree" has become the Inspirer? My friend Dallas inspired me to run my first

100-miler after she attempted her first. All three of my friends humanized what I thought were super-human feats. I have included insight from some of the first-timers that I have coached so that they can also help humanize the marathon for you. They were in your shoes at one time, albeit a different size and brand, but they were just as SCITED as you and they did it.

I had no idea how finishing a marathon would transform me. How it would give me that first jolt of confidence that I was searching for throughout my life. That marathon was the first time in my life that I was doing something outside of my comfort zone that no one else was telling me I had to do it. Not my parents, boss, professor, husband, friends, sibling, anyone. It was solely driven by me, myself and I. Completing my first marathon turned the "I can't" into "what else can I do?" Your first marathon will do the same for you. Especially if you doubt the achievement as much as I did. When was the last time you consciously did something that gave you a little angst in your gut? It's in those angst-laden moments when we are most alive and really showing up in our lives. On the other side of that angst is a soul transformation that you would have missed out on had you stayed in your comfort zone. I am sending you a virtual high five right now for just saying no to your own status quo.

The confidence I gained from that first marathon gave me the courage to try other "firsts" in my life. Some of those firsts included: an Ironman triathlon even though I am still afraid of open water, taking improv classes to get over my fear of public speaking, breaking off an engagement, running a 100-mile race even though I wasn't able to finish, saying "I love you" first when I didn't hear it back and sky diving to get over my fear of heights. One uber-courageous first happened just two years ago. On June 3rd, 2016, I left my six-figure job and 26-year career in accounting, to become a full-time running coach and Marathon Whisperer! I officially called this life changing decision, de-corporation! Had I not experienced so many SCITED firsts, I never would have found the courage to finally do something that I love, instead of doing something I thought I had to do.

It is normal to feel overwhelmed with the endeavor of running 26.2 miles for the first time. If you think about it, anytime we do something for the first time, it can be overwhelming because there are a lot of unknowns. Especially the possibility that we may not succeed. When this feeling comes upon you in training and on race day, I want you to think about other things that you have done in your life that you had to dig deep within to get through, whether it was something that you wanted badly or something that the universe unexpectedly brought your way. For example, have there been any relationships or jobs that you consciously had to walk away from? On the other end of the spectrum are there any jobs that you were let go from or break-ups you didn't see coming? Like me, did it take you four times to finally pass the CPA exam? Have you ever moved to a new city and started all over? Draw strength and courage from these types of experiences that you have gotten through that you didn't think you could. Draw strength from those emotionally challenging moments too that you just wanted to blink the pain of the loss away instead of letting time heal that wound. Capitalize on that resilience you gained!

I wrote this book for those of you who don't think you can do a marathon and for those of you who are signed up for your first marathon and are SCITED. I share my lessons learned from running over 100 marathons around the world. I also incorporate human RunSpiration in each mile of the book from my "no longer" first-timers.

Now, let's get you ready for your first marathon!

Meet First-Timer, Max D.

One word to describe my first marathon: Terrific

Prior to signing up for my first marathon, I had been a "jogger" all of my life. I would run 5 to 6 miles every day. This changed when I met Coach Denise as she educated me on how important it is to take days off to allow my body time to recover. Running helps me deal with the time zone changes when I travel for work. Yes, I still work. It keeps me young too. I jog for my health and in a big way for my psychology. I just feel better if I run a bit every day! I signed up for my first marathon to keep moving and to challenge myself, particularly in an endeavor that I admire.

Given my jogging regimen, I signed up for the marathon with the goal of completing just one. I'm proof that you're never too old to try anything new—my secret is mind over matter. It really is true. To train and complete a marathon, you must really want to do it. I believe that one can do anything if they really desire to do so.

Throughout my training, I did not really think about whether I would run another. I just wanted to complete one first. I completed my first, and now, I am already signed up to run my second. This time around I want to improve my time. On race day, especially in the latter miles, it was really tough. It felt like the finish line kept moving further and further away from me. I was beyond delighted though, when it was finally in sight and I was able to cross it!

In retrospect, one thing that really helped me throughout this journey was having Denise as a great, understanding, patient coach! We ran the whole marathon together from start to finish.

Mile 3: Feet Don't Fail Me Now!

Chapter focus: Gain an understanding of a marathon runner's best friend; running shoes.

Next to our raw, human grit, our shoes are the most important piece of equipment we will need on our journey to 26.2. There is a method to my madness in having this mile so early in my book. To help keep injury free and comfortable throughout your runs, it is critical that you are running in properly fit shoes. Your shoes provide support for the stress that your skeletal system sustains with every foot strike. When your foot hits the ground, your skeletal system is absorbing approximately three to five times your body weight. For a 150-pound runner, this translates to roughly 450 to 700 pounds! Running in a shoe with too much support or too little support for you, is an injury waiting to happen. Outside of smart watches, race fees, compression boots and wireless headphones, shoes will be the most expensive but also the most important investment you will make.

Got Fit?—I recommend that you go to a specialty running store to get fit for your running kicks. More than likely, your fit specialist will be a fellow runner who is experienced in the fit process. This will ensure that the shoes you are running in provide the correct amount of support for your foot's degree of pronation. In laymen's terms, pronation is the natural rolling inward or flattening of the foot that occurs when we run and walk. It aids shock absorption. Remember the story about the Three Bears? When it comes to your running shoes, you want to be in shoes that enable your foot to pronate "just right." If you pronate just right, you will want to stick with a neutral shoe. If you pronate too much, a stability shoe will help correct your natural tendency to over pronate. If you don't pronate enough—supinate—a motion control shoe will help correct your foot's tendency to under-pronate.

When going for your fit, it is a good idea to go sans-workout; meaning, do not go right after a run, bike ride or after standing on your feet all day. Test driving shoes with swollen feet, could lead to you coming home with shoes that are too big. It is recommended that your running shoes are at least a half size bigger than your everyday shoe to allow for the natural swelling from running. To determine your degree of pronation, the fit specialist will watch you run. It can also be helpful for the fit specialist, if you bring in your current running shoes even if they are old. That way, they can use the wear and tear on the sole of your foot as additional insight in selecting the right shoe for you. Once they determine what category of shoe you need; neutral, motion control, or stability, they will bring out various manufacture's models for you to try on. The specialist will recommend that you take the shoes for a run in the store or outside, weather permitting. As a guide, you should be able to have about a "thumb" space worth (from the thumb's knuckle to the tip of the thumb) of distance between your big toe and the tip of your running shoe. To make sure that you don't lose your runner card, avoid buying your shoes based solely on color. Fit trumps color here! One benefit with going to a specialty store for your shoes is that most of them are owned by runners and want you to keep running, be happy with your shoes and continue to shop with them. That being said, if you find that your new shoes are not comfortable after logging training miles, most stores will exchange the shoes and re-fit you for another pair of shoes that should be "just right". When replacing your shoes, you can usually find the prior version of your shoe on sale at race expos and online. I don't recommend using store bought insoles in your running shoes. If you want to go that route, I would suggest having professional orthotics by a podiatrist.

And I will run and run 500 miles—Just how long do running shoes last? On average, shoes will last for approximately 300-500 miles depending upon the surface area you run on. The softer your running terrain, the more miles you will be able to get out of them. One way to get even more miles out of your shoes is to alternate between two pairs of shoes in your training season. By allowing one pair of shoes to "recover" after a run and then grabbing the rested pair of shoes for your next run, you can get roughly 100 extra miles. One caveat with this mileage benchmark is in regards to running shoes that have low mileage on them but they are more than a year old. From the outside, they look brand, spanking new and ready to hit the road. On the inside, however, they have lost their durability and support structure. Personally, I can tell when it's time to replace my shoes when I start to feel the pavement, running path, treadmill more than usual on my run.

Garmin Connect™ has a cool feature that you can add a pair of your shoes to your profile and then define target mileage for those shoes. As you log your runs, there is a gauge on your dashboard that displays how many miles you have logged towards hitting this mileage target. Back in the day, I used to mark the purchase date of my new shoes on the shoe box and then monitor my mileage to date using my training log.

Meet First-Timer, Sarah C.

One word to describe my first marathon: Life-changing

Before registering for the marathon, I was new to running. I had done a few 5Ks and 10Ks but never took it very seriously. Running was something I enjoyed but the idea of a marathon seemed unachievable. In July 2014, my life was turned upside down in a matter of days. The person I thought I would spend the rest of my life with had left me. I was in shock. I went through the motions for weeks. I would wake up, shower (only when necessary...), go to work, go home, cry, drink wine, cry, sleep, rinse and repeat. If I had to be around people, I engaged long enough before I would go back home and continue to be sad by myself. I honestly didn't know what to do with myself. One minute, I had this beautiful life planned and the next minute, it had disappeared into the night. How was I supposed to move forward? How could I even begin to rebuild? And if I did, what would that even look like?

I'm a type A, plan every moment, color-coordinated calendar type, so for me it has always been important to set goals for myself. This period in my life was no different. I needed a win, something that would lift me up out of this funk. I craved something that would not only help me feel good about myself but would also give me something to look forward to. Twenty minutes with Coach Denise over coffee was the start of something incredible, but I don't think I fully realized it then. Her energy is contagious. When we met, I vividly remember her telling me that I was going to run the Chicago Marathon the following fall and for the first time since my life was sent into a tailspin, I was finally excited about something!

If you want to run a marathon, you can and you will. One of the greatest things about running is that everyone can do it. It doesn't matter how old you are, what kind of shape you are in, what your background is in and out of running. You will see all types of people out there. One of my favorite quotes is, "If you want to change your body, exercise. If you want to change your life, become a runner." I most definitely will run another, it's just a matter of deciding where and when.

If I could have a do over of my first marathon, I'd tell myself "don't stop to pee unless you absolutely have to."

Mile 4: Getting Your Syllabus

Chapter focus: Training for a marathon is just like taking a class. You receive a syllabus. You do your homework and then you take the final.

Before starting any fitness regimen, including Marathoning 101, I recommend that you first see a medical professional to obtain medical clearance. Prior to starting this class, I also recommend that you have a strong running base in which you can comfortably run a 4 to 6-mile long run and comfortably average 15 to 20 miles a week. Once you have these prerequisites checked off, we can officially start class! I have included two different training plans depending upon your current fitness level. My training plans are designed to allow for proper buildup of mileage each week and proper recovery between workouts. You can find the syllabus that is right for you in Aid Station 1.

    Life Happens—Training for a marathon is a huge time commitment and with time being one of our most precious commodities, there is a high probability that life will get in the way of completing some of your workouts. There will be days when work, kids, dentist appointments, theatre tickets, emergency vet visits, Cubs (representin'!) tickets, all of the above, etc. will get in the way of your training. Don't fret and automatically fast forward in your mind to a DNF (Did Not Finish) stamp for race day. A handful of missed workouts does not mean that you should throw in your race bib. However, one rule of thumb that I want you to follow throughout your training is to make sure that if you should miss any workouts, you do not to miss your long run. The long run is the most important run each week because it emulates the marathon the most. Some weeks, you may need to reschedule your long run from the weekend to a weekday or vice versa to ensure you get it in. Another rule of thumb to follow when you miss workouts is to not cram in the workouts that you missed on your off days. You don't want to cram for this final because the training plans allow for proper rest days and the proper long run mileage build-up each week. The scheduled rest days in the plans allow for your body and mind time to recharge. They are just as important as your training days.

Back in 2003, I was training for my first Ironman triathlon. I was SCITED beyond belief because the race included a 2.4-mile swim and I was and still am afraid of open water. I was so diligent with my training that I rarely missed a workout and rarely went out socially. I mistakenly believed that if I missed a workout I would not finish the triathlon. To this day, I still remember selling my ticket to a concert because I knew if I went to the concert, I would get very little sleep and be very dehydrated the next morning. This would resonate to a painfully tough and crappy morning swim session. Fifteen years later, I am still beating myself up that I chose a swim workout over seeing the Rolling Stones play at Comiskey Park. I even had a seat on the baseball field. During my first Ironman triathlon season, I was so stressed and overwhelmed, that I eventually had to get a mouth guard because I was grinding my teeth so much at night. Fast forward to my second Ironman triathlon in 2011. I did not stress about completing every workout. I even had a social life outsight of my training. Ironically, I even missed two complete months of training because of a non-running related surgery. My finish time was only 45 minutes slower than my 2003 race. Moral of the story is that missing a handful of workouts will not break your race day; it is the whole training season and your drive to finish that helps get you to the finish line.

One Skip, Two Skip, Three Skip, No Skip!—When you think about skipping your workouts remember that the more work and fight you put through in your training, then the less work and fight you will have to go through on race day. I recently learned that Norman Schwarzkopf had a more elegant way of saying this; "The more you sweat in peace, the less you bleed in war." Each mile that you log is conditioning your body and mind to handle marathon morning. I have clients that will follow my training plans to a "T" and then I have those that get in the bare bones minimum mileage. Even though they both may finish, the latter client is more than likely to hurt sooner in the race and will hurt longer in the days following the race. They also have a higher probability of get injured. When I have the conversation in my head about skipping a run, I remind myself how much better I will feel after my run, compared to how I will feel without the run. I also tell myself to just get out and run a couple miles. Once I get a couple miles in, I find that I feel so good that I want to keep running. I also remind myself that I do not want to bleed in war.

From my own personal experience, before I started working with a running coach, I basically trained for my marathons by running when I felt like running and for whatever distance I felt like that day. Come race day, it never failed that around mile 15, I would be in excruciating pain with each foot strike. The pain would progressively get worse as I mentally pushed through to the finish line. After finishing these coach-less guided marathons, I would also walk like Frankenstein for a week. Walking up a curb seemed like climbing Mt. Everest. Fast forward to when I train properly, I am able to run short, easy mileage the next day.

Meet First-Timer, Beau D.

One word to describe my first marathon:
Conquered

I started running at a very young age, tagging along with my older sister Valerie. When I couldn't keep up with her any longer, I'd sit along the path and wait for her to come back and then we would run home. It was our quality time together. She passed away at the age of 18 when I was 10. I was heartbroken and I stopped running. In college, I started running again: not a lot, but a little. Valerie had always wanted to, but never did run a marathon. After college, I decided to train for one to fulfill that dream in her place. When I finished, I cried because I had completed something that I never thought that I could do, but also because in a way, I helped accomplish my sister's dream. Consequently, feeling the sense of accomplishment that comes with such a feat, I thrived on it. I then finished another for myself. Now, I'm currently training for my fourth marathon.

Completing a marathon is overcoming limitations and proving that you can do anything - no matter what - if you work hard. I think most people are stronger than they think. Your body can do amazing things when you put your mind to it. I learned how important it is to have people you trust around you. Training is hard, but it is easier when have people around you and a coach like Denise who makes running fun. Some of the people I met from training are still very close friends. Through the training, I learned to never give up, what my limits are, but mostly, I learned how to power through and overcome those limits.

If I had a do over of my first marathon, I would have practiced what Coach Denise preached in regards to the marathon not really starting until Mile 20. I would have gone out slower like she recommended. I didn't fully understand what she meant until I had a difficult time in the latter miles of my marathon.

Mile 5: Does This Hydration Belt Go with this Visor?

Chapter focus: How to dress for comfort and performance in training and on race day.

One of the many things that I love about running is that it is a low investment sport. I.e. it does not require a lot of gear to participate. You just need a properly fit pair of running shoes and moisture wicking clothing from head to toe. No matter what temperature you are running in, you want to make sure that what you are wearing is breathable, chafe-resistant and most importantly comfortable. Similar to nutrition and footwear, finding the right shorts, tights, singlet, sports bra, visor etc. for you, will be a personal preference through your own trial and error.

Just Say No to Cotton—Back in my day, we did not have as many options available for running gear. In fact, I remember my running wardrobe consisted mainly of cotton t-shirts, thick sweatshirts and sweatpants. Even the race shirts back then were cotton. One of the most important rules with dressing for success, is to just say no to cotton. Cotton is not a good fabric to run in because it does not breathe; once cotton gets wet, it stays wet. This can lead to overheating in hot temperatures and to chills in cold temperatures. Wet clothes can also lead to unnecessary chafing. Second, in figuring out how to dress, I recommend adding 20-degrees Fahrenheit to the outside temperature that you will be running in. This additional 20-degree gauge is due to our body producing its own heat when we exercise.

Holy Hotness!—For hot weather training and racing gear, I recommend light colored, breathable clothing. I also recommend wearing sunglasses along with visor or a hat. I never used to wear a hat and sunglasses until my coach informed me that squinting causes tenseness in my face and therefore I am not in a relaxed state. The most important gear to wear outside no matter the temperature is of course sunscreen, preferably waterproof. For extra protection alongside your sunscreen, you can actually wear clothing that has UV Protection built in.

This Little Piggy—Finding the right pair of running socks is just as important as zeroing in on the right shoes. Trying to run on swollen, cramped or even blistered feet is no fun and can make or break a race. As mentioned earlier in this mile, just saying "no" to cotton also applies with running socks. When selecting the right socks for your ten piggies, look for fabric that has been designed to draw moisture away from your feet and provide adequate cushioning. If you are prone to getting cramps in your feet, you may want to try socks that have compression in them to increase circulation. I have been running in Balega® socks since my coach first introduced me to them in 2006.

Embrace the Chafe—As an additional layer of defense in preventing chafing and blisters, you may need to add a layer of ointment between your skin and your clothing. Products such as Body Glide™, Squirrel Nut Butter™ and even old school, Vaseline™ can do the trick. I recommend that you put your chafing brand of choice on your feet, on your thighs if you are running in shorts and for woman, under your sports bra seams. If you are running in the rain you will need to add even more of the product to these areas, if not re-add during your run or race.

Baby, It's Cold—For cold weather training and racing gear, I recommend that the clothing that is closest to your skin be made of merino wool fabric. This will help keep you warm and also absorb your sweat. The next layer on top that I recommend would be a breathable wind proof jacket or vest. I have had a lot of success with a brand called Icebreaker™ for merino wool pieces. Their clothing has kept me warm and dry when I ran marathons in Antarctica, Reykjavik and South Africa. The great thing about their gear is that you do not have to wash it that often as it does not absorb odor. It is also dual-purpose wear as it looks great with jeans. In regards to keeping my hands warm, I recommend wearing mittens instead of gloves. There is strength, I mean warmth in numbers with the former. When your fingers are together skin on skin, they insulate each other to keep your hands warmer than if your fingers were separated in a pair of gloves. I actually have a pair of what I call, "glittens", they are a combination of gloves and mittens all in one. These are great for when your hands get too warm, you can open up the top of the "glitten" to expose just your fingertips. When it's really cold out I will stuff hand warmers inside my "glittens". For cold weather hats, I still haven't found the perfect hat for all temperatures. When it's really cold, I will wear a beanie hat and then a knit hat on top of the beanie. When it's mildly cold, I will just wear a knit cap.

Meet First-Timer, Rachel C.

One word to describe my first marathon:
Ineffable

I didn't really have a running background when I started this whole marathon adventure. I didn't hate running, I was just apathetic towards it... until I had a typical quarter life crisis. I broke it off with the man that I thought I was going to marry. I had graduated, but was struggling to get a job. I felt totally and completely worthless. Luckily, I had a group of friends that recognized the dark place I was in, so when I mentioned I wanted to do a silly 5K, they were all in with total enthusiasm. A few races later, surrounded by the love of my friends, I realized I never wanted this feeling to go away: the finish line feeling of "I did this. It hurt and it was hard and I did it anyway."

Though this quarter life crisis inspired me to start running, my cousin, Noah, who has Cystic Fibrosis, inspired me to finish my first marathon. I ran, I fundraised, so that one day, he can breathe easy. When I thought I was dying and couldn't breathe, when I thought I had hit my wall, I remembered that he felt like that every day of his life...so I pushed harder. Now, I have plans to run a marathon on every continent, just like Coach Denise. It sounds ridiculous, but when you're running for someone other than yourself, someone who deserves support, it gets you farther than you can ever imagine.

Every week, I learned that I was capable of something that seemed impossible two weeks before. Either you run farther or faster than you ever thought you could, or your run sucks and you learn to listen to your body. Either way, you are learning about yourself in a whole new light. I learned I can push myself to unbelievable limits. I learned I hate getting up early but I love running in the morning. I learned my family will do anything to support me. I learned chafing can be more painful than any sprain. I learned that I can do anything I set my mind to. I learned that there is nothing more empowering than a finish line!

One thing that surprised me on race day was that I had no idea my feet could hurt so much. I honestly couldn't even look down for the last three miles because I was sure I had bled through my shoes. Turns out, 26.2 miles is hard on your feet. Go Figure!

Mile 6: That Is A Lot Of Work For A Free Banana

Chapter focus: What to eat before, during and after a run; translating that knowledge to your perfect race day menu.

Garbage in, Garbage Out—Throughout your training, you want to be conscious about what you are fueling your body with. When it comes to marathon nutrition, "garbage in equals garbage out". We want to make sure that we are fueling our engine with the proper grade of gasoline so that we will not end up on "E," so to speak. As your weekly mileage and your long runs start to build up, you are going to need additional nutrition to keep you fueled and to aid muscle recovery. What I have learned from my own training experience and from working with my clients is that there is no magic formula for the timing and the type of nutrition your body needs: everyone's body is different. What works for me may not work for you and vice versa. Race day nutrition is a science in itself because you are trying to find the perfect formula between having enough nutrition to keep you running strong while not having too much nutrition in your stomach which might cause Gastrointestinal (GI) issues.

In deciding what is best for you, there are two things to keep in mind. First, use each long run to figure out what you should eat and hydrate with the night before, the morning of, during and after your run. The timing of your nutrition is also key. Our long runs become practice quizzes, helping us identify the right formula we will then execute come race week! The second thing to keep in mind regarding nutrition is that if you are relying on course nutrition and hydration, become familiar ahead of time with what will be available and practice with it during your training runs.

When I ran my first marathon in 1994, the only endurance nutrition that I was aware of was a Powerbar™. I basically gnawed on a piece at a time during the marathon because I was afraid to lose a crown. In my early years of marathoning, my race day fuel strategy would be a cup of coffee and plain piece of toast for breakfast. During the marathon, I would have 6 gels as well as the water and the sports drink provided by the race. By the time that I crossed the finish line, I felt like a little kid who demolished their Halloween candy in one sitting. I would not be able to eat normal food for hours. Now, I have my race day routine perfected to a piece of dry toast and coffee before the race. A gel in the start corral and then Tailwind™ nutrition mixed with water throughout the race.

For race week and marathon eve, my recipe for success is hydrating throughout the week with Tailwind™ nutrition. Two nights before the race, I have pasta with marinara and chicken. The night before, I only have pasta with marinara. I avoid oils, butter and protein the night before as that increases the probability that I will have GI issues. After my marathon, I have Amino Vital Rapid Recovery™ powder mixed with water.

Food for Every Belly—Visit your local running store and/or race expo and you will see that we have a plethora of nutrition options to choose from such as gels, blocks, powders, drinks, dried fruits and sometimes homemade treats. There are even gluten-free, caffeine free and electrolyte-laden options available. There are so many brands and flavors of nutrition to choose from that it can be overwhelming. I recommend that you experiment on your runs with different forms and brands to figure out what works for you. You can also get advice from runners in your circle to see what they use. Some of my clients have a hard time "stomaching" energy gels or blocks. Instead, they use dry dates or raisins. When I ran the Paris Marathon in 2016, they actually had orange slices, sugar cubes, and raisins at all of the aid stations. One trick that I learned with taking gels on the run is to just take a little bit at a time once you open it. I used to squeeze the whole gel in my mouth and it was such a shock to my stomach.

Drink Up!—Proper hydration on your training runs and on marathon day are also critical to your performance. This includes taking in water and key electrolytes, including calcium, sodium, magnesium and potassium. Electrolytes are necessary for proper body functions and to prevent cramping. When we sweat, we are not just losing water, but we are also losing electrolytes. Taking in too much water throughout your long run and race can lead to a serious and sometimes fatal condition called hyponatremia. Just like there are numerous nutrition products for you to choose from, there are also a wide variety of electrolyte products to try. In deciding what product to use, I recommend choosing a product which contains the key electrolytes and gets along with your stomach.

To help with recovery especially after races, long runs and your marathon, it is recommended that you hydrate and fuel your body with nutrition that is 4-parts carbohydrate and 1-part protein. Studies have shown that muscles are most receptive to rebuilding glycogen (stored glucose) stores within 20-30 minutes after you complete your run or race. I used to have chocolate milk as my recovery go-to. It fulfills the recommended carbohydrate and protein ratio and as an added bonus, it is yum in the tum! I have had a lot of success with recovery powders such as Amino Vital Recovery and Tailwind Rebuild a lot more effective. Again, what works for me, may not work for you and vice versa, so practice, practice, practice.

For my fellow coffee drinkers out there, I have an additional trick of the trade for you that I learned when I trained for my first Ironman triathlon. I know it might be hard, but I recommend that you give up coffee at the start of the training season or even the month before your marathon. That way, come marathon morning, when you are finally united with coffee again, you will experience a real jolt!

Meet First-Timer, Ademola A.

One word to describe my first marathon:
Enlightening

Before training for the marathon, I mostly ran just to stay in shape. As part of my regular routine, I would usually run 20-30 minutes on the treadmill, but my farthest distance before I started training for the marathon was only 5 miles. That was in 2011. Where I live, the Chicago marathon passes right in front of my house. So, in 2015, inspired by my wife, Danielle, I decided to run the marathon. I also did it as a way to challenge myself.

If someone who wanted to run a marathon didn't believe that they could, I'd say that running a marathon is very possible as long as you train well for it. Start training early, talk to someone who has experience running a marathon, like Coach Denise and stick to a training plan. After the marathon, I realized that the thought of 26.2 miles is no longer scary to me. Race day, I had a plan to run my own race and not get carried away by other runners going faster than I was. My goal was to complete the race and see the city of Chicago. I didn't think I would run another marathon at first. However, now I know I can improve on my time and plan to challenge myself and run more of them.

Throughout training, I realized I prefer to run in the mornings before the sun is out, I run faster when I run with a group, I am less sore when I stretch and foam roll after my runs. It looks like my first marathon inspired my wife, Danielle. In 2017, we both ran the Chicago marathon together from start to finish line.

After running my first marathon, I realized that having a strategy in place ahead of time helps you to run your own race.

Mile 7: Check Yo' Self

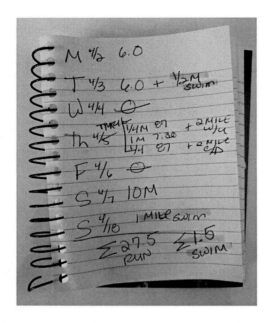

Chapter focus: How to keep yourself accountable throughout this 20-week semester

I believe that the marathon is so soul enriching because of the fact that no one else is telling you to do it. Your marathon is ignited and fueled by your own free will and want. You are not running a marathon because your boss, partner, parent, teacher, friend, neighbor, therapist, "fill in the blank", etc. told you that you had to run one. Most responsibilities in our lives, like our day to day obligations, stem from these parties and more. Not the marathon. It is all you! Whether you finish or not, you are the only person you have to report back to. Of course, we will share our marathon journey with everyone we come into contact with but this RunVenture is all you! So how do you keep yourself committed mile after mile after mile? No, there isn't an accountability app for that but below you will find some of my tricks of the trade for staying accountable to yourself.

Put Me in Coach—If you are the type of person who can execute against a training plan without having to check in with another person, then a marathon coach may not be necessary. If you however, are more likely to execute on your training plan if you have someone to report back to daily or weekly, then I recommend getting a coach. Even if you are self-driven enough to follow a training plan but know that you will have a lot of questions around pacing, nutrition, injury prevention, etc., then having a coach may also benefit you on your road to 26.2. When I train for a triathlon, I work with a coach because my default workout is to want to run, run, run. By having a coach to report my workouts to, I am more inclined to hit the pool and the bike.

Hear Ye! Hear Ye!—You know the saying, "what you put out to the universe, the universe will bring back to you?" Well, it holds true when it comes to you nervously, proudly and "scited-ly" advertising to your world that you are running your first marathon! Once you proclaim that commitment out to your world, you will have friends, family, your barista and everyone in the surrounding perimeter likely to ask you, how your training is going. You may even have to educate some of these accountability buddies on exactly how far a marathon is and be prepared to hear, "I don't even drive that far!" Knowing that there is even a 1 percent chance that someone in your circle is going to ask you about your marathon is the extra motivation you will need to get out the door on those days when you just want to ix-nay that run-ay! I encourage you to use your social media channel(s) of choice to share your journey to 26.2. You can share everything from your struggles, triumphs, post-run rewards, embarrassing moments from your training runs and races. Come marathon morning, this accountability squad will be especially eager to follow along as you achieve something that you once thought was out of reach. Personally, I would love to follow your journey so please tag me in your posts using #meyouand262 and @meyouand262. My hidden agenda with your sharing of your marathon training and race day with your accountability buddies is that you will more than likely inspire them to do a marathon; you will humanize it for them.

What You Measure is What You Get—From my own experience, keeping a training log definitely helps me stay in check. Even though I have a GPS smart watch that captures my run statistics, I just can't break up with a hard copy, manual entry training log. I am a visual person and need to see week to week how I am progressing through my training. To me, training data gets lost in the virtual world wide web.

I use a spiral notebook to log my workouts. The photo at the beginning of this Mile is actually one of the pages from my training journal. A single page represents a week. I add the Initial of the day of the week down the left side of the page. To the right of the day, I log my total mileage and any cross-training workouts completed. The latter is to keep me accountable with workouts that I would rather skip and run instead. When I run a race or do a track workout, I will also add my mileage splits and/or average pace. What happens with journaling my workouts is that week to week, when I see too many zeros on a page or zero cross training days, I get my butt out the door or to the gym. On the opposite end of the accountability spectrum, when I see a high mileage week or a PR at a race or workout, I give myself an atta-girl! I also highlight "fridge-worthy" workouts; those that are worth posting on your fridge! Remember in grade school when your parents would put one of your drawings or even your report card on the fridge? Just because we aren't five anymore doesn't mean we don't have "fridge-worthy" accomplishments in adulthood. When I set a personal record (PR) or complete a cross training session, I highlight that day's work out with a highlighter. It is easy to lose sight of how far you have come. That is why I also recommend going through your training log the night before your 20+ mile run and your marathon. Your training log becomes a great source of inspiration.

Fear of Running Alone (FORA)—Even after decades of marathoning, I still have mornings in which I just want to get a few more z's. Especially when double-digit mileage is on my to-do, I mean, to-run list. My alarm will go off and as conditioned as Pavlov's dog, I immediately think, "one more hour!", "just give me one more hour!" or even better, "two more hours and I promise that I will run later!" This sounds wonderful, right? This short-term reward comes with a hefty price. That price is something that I call the Fear of Running Alone (FORA). One symptom of FORA is having to mentally get through your run with you, yourself and your own vices. Compare this to having met up with your "reeps" (Running Peeps) and the miles pass by semi-effortlessly as you share random conversations. Your feet just follow your brain, right? Not to mention, we usually run faster and are less likely to short change a workout when we run with others. A more ego-striking price is knowing that those early birds that caught the run will be finished, fed, showered and seizing the rest of their day before you even start your run! Ouch, that will leave a mark. I only had to have FORA hit me a couple of times before I have learned to concede to my alarm clock and get my butt out the door to meet my reeps (running peeps).

Meet First-Timer, Alex J.

*One word to describe
my first marathon:
Amazinghardscaryemotionalthrilling*

Before training for the marathon, I had exercised regularly but rarely ran. At first, training gave me a way to deal with grief. I had a miscarriage after 11 weeks on June 3, 2014. I needed a tangible goal to achieve and the 2014 Chicago Marathon provided a great opportunity. It was a way to deal with my sadness. That was when I learned that running truly can be meditative. I have always loved a challenge but this was a challenge like no other I had ever taken on. I realized that I can push myself to amazing places.

I have found that runners come in all different shapes and sizes. If you think you can't, think again. You absolutely can. The experience—the training and the race—provides a natural high that feels amazing. I continue to be inspired to run for my children that are not here with me, and for my son who is. I was bitten by the bug the moment that I crossed the finish line for the first time. As of this writing, I am weeks away from running my first Boston Marathon.

One thing that I learned on race day that escaped me throughout my training runs, was that there is no such thing as a sports bra that doesn't cause chaffing, so stop spending money on them and just grin and bear it!

Mile 8: All About That Pacing

Chapter focus: How to use a "talk test" to set your pacing and why "slow" is a four-letter word that should be removed from your running vocabulary.

No "S" Bombs, Please—Before I talk about pacing, I want to preface it with a caveat. The caveat is as a Runner of Denise (ROD), you are not allowed to drop "S" bombs by describing yourself or your running as "Slow." To me, the slowest runner is the person still at home not trying. Outside of this slow population, everyone else is faster than them. The fact that you even have the self-discipline to get out there when you could just as easily choose not to, should warrant some accolades. Personally, walkers are not even slow to me because they are still moving forward and doing more than the person sitting on the couch. The athlete in front of the race sweep vehicle may be the last one to cross the finish line but if you think about who is really last in the race, it is again, all of the people who didn't show up on race day to try.

I stopped describing my workouts and race times as slow when I had an epiphany during one of my group track workouts. I was running warm up laps on the track when one of the guys in the group lapped me. His warm up pace was essentially my race pace. What the What? "If only,

I could be as fast as him," I thought. That got me thinking that maybe the runners behind me would love to be my "slow" because my warm up pace is their race pace! When we say we are slow, we are discounting the efforts and goals of runners that are striving for our "slow" paces. That is why I think slow is a bad word. It is a four-letter word after all. Not to mention, we never know if the runners ahead of us have more years of running practice than us, have been gifted with better genetics then our gene pool gifted us, have fire in their belly from something that happened or just happened to them.

The summer of 2015, I ran a back to back marathon and half-marathon in one weekend. On Saturday, I paced two of my clients in a marathon and then on Sunday I volunteered as a "sweeper" at a half-marathon. A "sweeper" stays with the last athlete in a race to make sure they safely make it from the start to the finish line. At the marathon, I ran alongside my clients, Kim and Fiona. Kim was shooting for her first Boston Qualifying (BQ) time while Fiona was looking to improve her qualifying time. The six months leading up to the race, they ran more mileage and more speed workouts then they had before. They had the mental and physical strength to BQ. Throughout all of the training runs, they were together stride for stride. They were more than ready for this race. They ended up making a pack before the marathon started that if one of them felt stronger, the other could go ahead and break up the band. About mile 12, the band broke up. Fiona was having a tough time and told us to go ahead. I stayed with Kim. I knew since I met Kim that she had Boston in her. She has a fight something fierce. I remember telling her in the latter miles, you have given child birth twice, this marathon has nothing on you! Still not sure if this helped or hurt her. About mile 21, Fiona came up behind us and passed us. I won't lie, when that happened, there was crying in marathoning! I cried proud tears for both of them. They didn't hit their overall goal but I saw them give more than I had ever seen in their training. Kim ended up running her fastest marathon and Fiona dug deep after having a rough first half of the race. I am still proud of both of these ladies. The following day, I "swept" a local half-marathon. I stayed with the last finisher. She was 60 years old and had recently lost over 100 pounds. Not once did she say, she couldn't do it, that she wanted to stop or that she was hurting. She stayed in the game and didn't quit. We made it to the finish line with just the race staff waiting for us. Everyone else was gone. Her finish time was five hours and twelve minutes. I was just as proud of her as I was Kim and Fiona!

Regardless of the clock time these three women received, I saw the same raw, human grit in each of them. They didn't win their races so they must be slow, right? Nope, they gave their best and pushed through when thoughts of quitting ran through their head.

Need Oxygen!—They say that the devil is in the details, however, when it comes to pacing your runs, I disagree. A lot of my clients will ask me for details wanting to know what pace they should run in each of their workouts. Instead of giving them a particular mile pace to hit, I have them run their workout based upon effort. After all, when Pheidippides ran from Marathon to Athens to announce Greece's underdog victory over the Persians, he was not wearing a Timex™ let alone an Apple™ watch to monitor his pace.

For me, my gauge to use for effort-based training is my ease or struggle to talk during my run. I basically have three descriptors on my gauge: "conversation" pace, "need oxygen" pace and "talk more but not want to" pace. The latter two descriptors will come into play when I run a speed workout or when I race. At a high level, speed workouts involve running shorter distances (intervals) really fast while allowing a rest period between the intervals. Speed workouts will be covered in more depth in Mile 19.

- When I have an easy run, warm up or cool down mileage, I will run a pace that I can comfortably talk the whole time. This is my **"conversation pace."**

- When I am racing a 5K or running quarter mile intervals in a track workout, I should only be able to emit from my lips, **"need oxygen."** My breathing is so taxed at this pace, that these are the only two words that I can utter, while at the same time, they appropriately reflect what I am wishing for.

- When I am running longer interval distances (mile and two-mile intervals) or longer race distances such as a 10K or a half-marathon, I am able to speak a **"longer sentence"** than "need oxygen" but not want to speak that often.

- For the "need oxygen" pace and the "longer sentence" pace, I lock into a pace that is "manageably-uncomfortable."

No matter the pace that I am running, I focus on keeping my breathing controlled versus all over the board. My breathing becomes rhythmic. In running and in life, the one thing that I can control is my breathing. The distance that I am running then determines that degree of taxation so to speak, that my breathing will be. For instance, if I am running a 5K my breathing will be a lot more taxed than if I were running a half-marathon. The degree of taxation is inversely related to the distance of the run.

When Being Negative is a Positive—When it comes to running the marathon, so many of us are guilty of running too fast out of the start gate; myself included. It's a natural reaction to do this. Your legs are rested from tapering for three weeks. Your adrenalin meter is on full force as you are about to do something you have never done before. The energy of the crowd makes you feel like you are the Grand Marshall of this electrifying, human-will fueled parade.

But I caution you to slow your roll. They say that the best way to run a marathon is by running either the same pace throughout or by running the second half of the marathon faster than the first half. The latter approach, which is called negative splitting, is what I strive for in all of my races, regardless of the distance. It wasn't until I ran my first negative split marathon that I FINALLY believed the experts. Before this epiphany, I was the queen of positive splitting. I would train hard all season, hitting 95 percent of my workouts. Come race day, I would toe the line and take off like a horse out of the gate. Boom, I would hit the first six to eight miles around 9:10 minute mile pace. Then as I hit my wall, I start getting passed by most of the runners that I had I passed in the early miles. I was just served a big ole piece of humble pie! Not to mention, my pace progressively slowed down more and more. In those latter miles, I would fight to hold a 12 minute per mile pace. After the marathon, I would be so disappointed in myself that I sacrificed a season of hard work by not running a smart race.

When I first started marathoning, I didn't know anything about pacing. I didn't even wear a watch. The first season that I trained with Coach Greg. I ran with a pace group during the marathon. I picked up a pace bracelet at the expo and then I met up with the 3:40 pace group in the start corral. As the mile markers kept coming up, I noticed I was hitting the times on the bracelet mile after mile. I think it was in the last 2 miles that I broke away from the pace group and crossed the finish line with a 3:37! That night I called my friend, Ken and told him what I did. I told him I just followed a bracelet the whole time and hit my goal time. He said, Denise, "that's called pacing!" I hung up the phone a tad embarrassed but also excited I knew the secret to racing smart.

Marathon morning, you get to decide. Would you rather be the passer in the latter miles or in the early miles? Slowing down takes practice and patience. I promise it will be worth it in the long run (pun intended) if you run a consistent pace or a negative split pace race. Negative split race means that you run the second half of the race faster than the first half. We know the whole race is physical, right? We also know that when we hit our wall, the marathon becomes more mental than physical. Knowing the latter, wouldn't you rather have a little spring left in your step to help counteract the "why did I sign up for this?" and "who moved my finish line" playlist playing in your head.

To help you slow down your roll in the marathon, here are some of my tricks of the trade that have worked for me:

1. Once you cross the chip mat, take off at a pace that is slower than what you would normally run. The way to test this "reserved" pace is to consciously and continually ask yourself, can I go faster? If you answer, "yes", you are going the right pace. High fives to you! Don't get too excited though from my high fives and then pick up the pace. If you answer, "no", you are going too fast and may be setting yourself up for a positive split. Bring your pace down. Don't speed up until you feel that you can hold that faster pace all the way through to the finish

line. Even if this means that you don't bring up your pace until mile 20 in the marathon or mile 16 in your 20+ miler. It's hard to say exactly what mile this will occur at because it is so personal. This also takes practice, so don't beat yourself up if it you don't get it right away.

2. Before you toe the start line, make sure that you know your 5K and 10K pace per mile. Now that you know how fast you can run a 5K and a 10K, do not run this pace until the last 5K and 10K of the marathon. This is coming from my own experience. I used to run so fast for the first 10K and then fight to even run my 20-miler pace the last 10K.

3. If the race provides pacers, start off with a pace group that is slower than your goal pace. Stay true to this pace until you know you can break away from the group and hold that pace. Just like pace strategy number 1 above, you do not want to speed up too early. That is the worst when you break ahead of the pace group only for them to pass you later on (again, this is from my own humble experience). What is important about running with a pace group is that the marathon is your race, so don't give the reins completely to the pacers. Know your pace and be OK holding back if they start out too fast. This just recently happened to me at a local marathon. I started with the 3:55 pace group because my race goal was actually 3:40. Right out of the gate, they were doing 8:35 mile splits when we should have been at an 8:57 mile pace. I asked my pace group mates if they were also getting 8:35 miles and they confirmed. I dropped behind and no one else joined me. At one point, my group was more than a half mile ahead of me. It was mile 11.6 when I passed them. Shortly thereafter, I also passed the 3:50 marathon pace group.

4. If you normally run to music, try starting your long run or your marathon without music. Don't turn on your music until the run or race becomes more mental than physical. Another

option is to start the race with an e-book or a podcast and then in those mentally-dependent miles, switch to your music. I have a client who listens to movies on her long runs and on race day. These options will definitely keep you starting at a reserved pace. See how I didn't "S" bomb there? During my marathons, I start off with a podcast or an old playlist. Then, when I want to "drop the hammer", I switch to my dance music and even more powerful, a new playlist of dance songs.

Throughout all of these approaches, you will have a competitive advantage of having more spring in your step compared to those runners that started too fast out of the gate.

Take a Walk

A lot of runners give walking a bad rap. I used to. When I first starting marathoning, I would question why someone would walk during a race. It's a race people! I just had to be passed by a few run/walkers to realize that they had something on me. In those early marathons, it never failed that my knees would lock up about mile 21. Each foot strike then became excruciating. My knees probably locked up due to the fact that they were in continual motion for four plus hours. Now that I add walk breaks during my marathons it breaks up that momentum and I no longer have that pain. In the marathons that I race, I speed walk 30 seconds at each aid station. If I am racing a hilly course, my walk breaks become the uphill sections. Two important things to remember about walking are one, you need to walk when you want to and not when you have to. Two, walk as if you have to go to the bathroom and you can't find the bathroom. Regarding the former, if you wait until you have to walk it's too hard to restart running. Make sure to add those walk breaks when your legs are still fresh. For the latter, you will find that your "can't find the bathroom" pace is very close, if not faster, than your "run the whole marathon" pace especially in the latter miles. If you don't already do a walk/run interval, I recommend that you practice taking walk breaks in your long runs. Especially during your 20-mile training run.

Meet First-Timer, Sean D.

One word to describe my first marathon:
Exhilarating

In 2013, I was 30, ate a lot of unhealthy food, smoked two packs of cigarettes a day and weighed 300 pounds. I had run one complete mile in high school, and it was one of the hardest things I had ever done. A friend of mine had lost about 80 pounds with the help of a medically supervised weight loss program. I decided in January of 2014 that I would do the same thing and went on to lose 75 pounds in three months. At that point I was advised to start doing some exercise, so I got on the treadmill. At first, a 1/4 mile was difficult, but I took advice, slowed down, and worked up to one complete mile and kept setting more goals. By the end of 2015, I had run three half-marathons, had lost 110 pounds total, was lifting five or six days a week, was biking and was up for any new challenges. My friend Gordon had run several marathons and he inspired me to take the plunge. His description of running in marathons made it all seem worth the time and the effort.

In my old way of thinking, I had a long list of nevers. One thing on this list was that I would never run a marathon even though I had run three half-marathons. Then Coach Denise posted on social media that the Chicago marathon was open for lottery registration. I decided to enter and I got in. Through the experience, I learned that I am a runner. I always felt like I was an impostor, not a real runner. As it turns out, anyone can become a runner. Almost anyone can run a marathon, given that they train physically and mentally beforehand. You don't have to run the 26.2 miles on day one of training--that would truly be impossible for most. Instead, it's one training run at a time. Broken up into pieces, it is very obtainable. I loved running my first marathon around my home city of Chicago -- I hope to do it again in a few years. I'm excited to run my next marathon in New York.

In running my first marathon, I learned that the amount of time and effort I put into training and recovery was directly proportional to the amount of pain that I had experienced on race day.

Mile 9: Not Running Really Sucks!

*Chapter focus: The importance of listening to your body, cross training and strength training to help
stay injury free.*

Just Keep on Swimmin' & Liftin'—If you are like me, you do not want running taken away from you. All you have to do is get sidelined once with an injury and you will be preaching loudly to me in the choir! There is a reason why they sell shirts at race expos touting that running is cheaper than therapy! One of the ways that I have been able to keep run, run, running for over 3 decades is by incorporating cross training workouts into my marathon training routine. You will notice in the training plans in Aid Station 1, that I designate cross training days for you. I recommend your cross-training session last from 45 minutes to an hour. Swimming, yoga, and pilates are all examples of low impact cross training options. Biking, provided it does not included intense climbing or intense speed, is also a good cross training option. Even though you are still active, these cross-training options give your legs a much-needed break while at the same time they help you become a more "muscularly -diverse" runner instead of just a "quad centric" runner. When I don't want to swim, because let's face it, running is more fun, I remind myself that the more I swim, the more that I can run. As a side note, swimming is also a great option for active recovery the day after your long run. Moving your legs against the water's resistance loosens up tight muscles without any impact on your joints. For my fellow music lovers, note that there are water proof music players to help the yards and meters go by. I rarely swim without my music player, except of course when I am swimming in open water.

Penalty Flag—I cannot stress enough the importance of listening to your body to help prevent injuries. You know your body the best so watch for when it throws you a penalty flag. For me, when I have a strange feeling or ache in a joint, muscle or body part that lingers for more than two weeks, I seek out a professional. Especially if the pain still lingers or has gotten worse after giving my body proper rest. Again, this goes back to me not wanting running taken away from my daily routine. I would rather have a professional prognosis and plan of attack than mistaken self-diagnosis. The latter usually results in more time off rehabbing than if I went straight to the expert upon the flag toss. Knock on wood, I have only been sidelined by two major injuries. One injury occurred in 2003 and resulted from wearing cheap, support-less boots to work all day. The next day it felt like someone dropped a dresser on my arch. I ended up breaking a bone in my foot which led me to having to wear a custom orthotic. I am probably one of the few marathoners out there wearing an orthotic because of a fashion injury! My other injury resulted from the car accident on August 16, 2009. I broke five vertebrae in my back. Season after season, I will have a lot of friends and clients that keep running through an injury and then end up making their injury worse. I blame this on the juxtaposed implications fueled by the power of the mind: our best friend and our worst enemy. It is our best friend when it helps us push through those last few miles of the marathon when our legs just want to quit. It is our worst enemy when it helps us push through those last few miles of the marathon when we have pulled a muscle, dangerously escalated heart rate, minor stress fracture, low electrolytes, etc. It's best to seek out the help of a professional when we need to differentiate between the two types of scenarios.

Method to My Madness—Two additional causes of running related injuries are doing too much running too soon or not allowing proper recovery between hard workouts. Back in Mile 4, we touched on your Marathoning 101 syllabus. The two training plans that I have included allow for proper recovery time between hard workouts as well as allowing for the proper buildup of your mileage week to week. I define a hard workout as a long run, a race and/or a speed workout. You want to minimize doing these types of workouts back to back. I recommend that you stick to your syllabus as best you can.

Which Way to the Beach?—In addition to cross-training, strength training is another great way to minimize injury and make you a stronger runner. Even if you do not have a gym membership or do not want to spend the money on a personal trainer, there are plenty of exercises we can call upon from high school gym class, that you can do to make you a stronger, injury free runner. Can you say, burpees, push-ups, sit ups, wall sits, etc.? If you work with a personal trainer or strength coach, make sure to let them know that you are also training for a marathon. That way, they will be able to target your weak and/or out of balance muscle groups. One caveat with strength training is to make sure that you do not work your legs on the same days that you also do a hard workout. I actually do my strength training during my fitness classes. There is a studio by my house that combines great dance music, a circuit of treadmill running mixed with a circuit of free weights and your own body weight on the floor. These workouts are dual purpose because I get mileage and strength training in in one sitting.

Meet First-Timer, Ben D.

One word to describe my first marathon:
Amazing

I had done a good amount of running in my life before I trained for marathons because of my background in sports. I played competitive tennis in high school and college. While watching some friends run the New York City Marathon in 2014, I spotted tennis player Caroline Wozniacki running it. It was so inspiring because she ran the marathon while she was still competing on the tour. I thought to myself, if my friends *and* a top ten tennis player in her prime of her tennis career can run a marathon, then I can do it too. I wanted to face a challenge that I have never faced before that involved physical and mental strength. Even more, I wanted to use the opportunity to help save animals, so I signed up to run and raise funds for Team PAWS Chicago. I have four pets that are rescues and there are many great animals who deserve to have long, happy and healthy lives.

I know lots of people start training with a lot of doubt in their minds. Focus on that "Yes you can" feeling. Anything is possible. You can surprise yourself. On the day of the marathon, you will feed off all the energy from the crowd. Before I even finished my first marathon, I knew I wanted to run another. I've already run three marathons and am now training for my fourth. Thanks to 4:00 AM runs, I have learned how disciplined and tough I can be from my training. I also learned how much I really wanted it—nothing was going to stop me. On race day, I learned that anything is possible and I can achieve great things with hard work.

In looking back at my first marathon, I wish I knew that it would be a "marathon" just getting to the NYC Marathon start line on Staten Island.

Mile 10: My Legs Are Hungover

Chapter focus: The importance and different types of recovery that will keep you marathon ready.

What you do after your run is just as important as what you do during your run. This is especially the case as the weekly mileage accumulates and the long runs start to get into the double digits. To minimize those days in which you start a run and your legs already feel as heavy as concrete or you feel like you lost your mental mojo to even get out the door, draw from some of my recovery tools below:

Rest Days—My training plans include rest days that allow your body time to repair and recharge from the stress that training has put it through. Running too many days in a row without any days off will increase your chance of getting injured. Rest days also help minimize mental burnout.

Ice Baths—For my runners that train with me through the summer months, part of our post workout routine includes a treatment at "Mother Nature's Cryotherapy" office. After our long runs, I have my runners stand in Lake Michigan for at most 15 minutes with the water level up to their mid-thigh. The ice-cold water helps reduce inflammation, flushes out waste products and once the tissue warms, there is increased blood flow that helps give the healing process a jump start. When you don't have access to a cold lake, you can also fill your tub with a couple of bags of ice and cold water. I recommend that for indoor do-it-yourself ice baths, you layer up on top with warm clothes and listen to your favorite playlist or podcast to help distract you from the cold.

The lake freeze has helped me bounce back from some of my hardest workouts and races. After my first 100-mile finish in November of 2017, I ended up standing barefoot in Lake Michigan for 15 minutes while wearing 2 layers of Icebreaker merino wool on top and my hooded ski jacket as the outermost layer. I also put my latest dance playlist on to help transport me mentally to warm, fun thoughts. Can you believe I had the whole lake to myself? After my lake freezes my legs felt phenomenal.

Puppies! Pizza!—As your weekly mileage starts to build up, it's important to start adding deep tissue massage to your training regimen. I learned about massage late in my marathoning game. I had probably run about 17 marathons before I got my first massage. I had a misconception that massages were about relaxation, rainbows and unicorns so I avoided them every season. I did not see the need or the cost justification. That was until I trained for my first Ironman triathlon in 2003. My triathlon buddies boasted about how much massages had helped them get through the 10-plus weekly hours of training. Ever since then, I have my massage therapist on speed dial. During marathon season, I get them every 3-4 weeks. If you don't know who to go to for massage, ask one of your fellow runners or even the staff at your local running store who they go to. Some races even have massage therapists at the finish lines offering complimentary massages. Like finding the right shoes, you may need to experiment until you find the right massage therapist. After your massage, you want to make sure that you hydrate to help flush out the toxins that were released from the massage. You also want to make sure that you do not work out afterwards as this will counteract the work that your massage therapist just put you through. I won't lie when I get my deep tissue massages, they hurt. They don't hurt the whole time but my therapist finds spots that make me want to go to my happy place. That is when I say, "Puppies and Pizza!" during the massage.

Foam Rolling—Foam rolling is also key to speeding up muscle repair after workouts. Think of foam rolling as do-it-yourself deep tissue massage. Applying moderate pressure at the point of contact between the roller and your muscle will help break up scar tissue and adhesions between the muscles, bones and skin. Foam rolling—myofascial release—also increases blood flow to the area which aids recovery.

Recovery Fuel—After running a long run or a race, you want to replenish your muscles as quickly as possible with a 4-part Carbohydrate and 1-part Protein drink or meal. This doesn't just help repair our muscles but it also helps restore our energy. To be most effective, you want to take in your recovery nutrition of choice within 20-30 minutes of finishing your run/race. It's during this timeframe, that muscles are most receptive to rebuilding glycogen (stored glucose) stores. This will help minimize muscle stiffness and soreness. Nutrition bars, a bagel with peanut butter or a smoothie made with fruit and yogurt are good options. For me, once my runs get longer than 2 hours or I do an intense training session, I use Amino Vital Recovery powder or Tailwind Rebuild powder. I alternate between the two products depending on what flavor I want to treat myself to. They have been my go-tos for bringing the spring back into my step. I don't feel the effects of these powders immediately, it's more my legs don't feel like "concrete" the next day like they used to post long run.

Meet First-Timer, Emily L.

One word to describe my first marathon: Emotional

Growing up the tallest in my class, I looked like an athlete so every coach in the school was always trying to get me to join their team—until they saw my complete lack of hand-eye coordination. Since you don't need to be able to catch or throw to run, my dad really encouraged me to take up cross-country because he thought I could be good. I hated it. The next year, I tried out for cheerleading because the seasons overlapped—now I didn't have to run. Sorry dad. It wasn't until a decade later I was living abroad after college without internet, television, or many books that I decided to pick up running to pass the time. I ran for the next few years on and off.

I'm great at coming up with excuses to not run - painful knees, clicking hips, a sleep disorder, the cough I get whenever it's chilly, these are just a few. Living in Chicago, though, it's hard to ignore the marathon and every year I would feel that pull to sign up. In 2017, my brother in-law Dan and I signed up to run for the Chicago Lights Charity Team. They then set me up with Coach Denise who came along with a community of supportive people that made running so fun. Fast forward into the training season and I was hopping out of bed early on Saturdays for our group long runs.

Through my training, I learned that I'm much more capable of completing a challenge when I surround myself with the right people. I was continuously inspired throughout training, by everyone who supported my charity, my friends and family who joined me for runs and cheered me on at races, the physical therapists who changed my experience of running completely, and my coach, Denise and fellow runners who kept me accountable and made me want to show up. I've never felt stronger than when I was training for the marathon and plan to continue to run. Dan didn't end up getting to run (For the best reason - my niece was born later marathon day!) so I'm excited to train again with him for next year's Chicago marathon. This time he is going to run it too!

If I could do my first marathon over, I'd watch my pace more closely the first half. It was just so easy to get caught up with the excitement, I didn't leave anything for the second half.

Mile 11: Map My Fun

Chapter focus: Ways to have fun on your run.
Yes, you heard that right, running is fun!

Training Mates—So how do you get through your 20 weeks of run, run, runnin' without getting bored to tears or mentally burned out? For me, it's all about having a variety of training partners to run with. Who I bring on my run depends upon where my head is at pre-run. If I have a lot on my mind and need to clear my head, I will hit the pavement with just me, myself and I. It is amazing how much clarity and reflection I get on these solo runs that I would not receive if I stayed stagnant in thought. If I want to be educated, inspired or amused, I will listen to a podcast or an audio book. Some of my favorite podcasts are NPR's *How I Built This*, Oprah's Super Soul Conversations, *Tim Ferris*, and *10 Junk Miles*. If I want to run faster than conversation pace, I listen to dance songs and get caught up in the fast beat. When I race a marathon, I only listen to about 8 songs, as I find one song and keep repeating it until I am ready for the next fast song. I then repeat that song until I am ready for a new one. Another option to help get through my miles is to run alongside my reeps (running peeps). On these runs, the miles go by quickly because we are so caught up in conversation. In one of my early marathons, I was also preparing for the CPA exam. I didn't feel right taking a whole day of studying away just to run a marathon, so I ran with my cassette player of my favorite teacher's lecture. When I hit my mental wall, I put her lecture on. I could hear her passion in her voice and she actually made auditing fun. I guess I was podcasting before we had podcasting. Lastly, there will also be runs in which I don't want to think at all and I just want to be present. On those runs and even during some of my marathons, I run naked, so to speak. No watch, no electronic distractions, just the scenery and sounds that are around me.

EPH- Experiences Per Hour—One huge take away or gift for that matter from my car accident is that I became more focused on the journey of my running instead of the destination During races, I would always see spectators holding a sign that read, "There will come a day when you cannot run and today is not that day" but it didn't hit home until my car accident almost took running away from me. Now, when I see that sign, I feel it in my heart and soul that today is a gift. This race is a gift. Running is a gift. My health is a gift. I don't know if it's part being older and wiser but when I reflect on my running journey in my final days, I will not remember my clock times, age group placements, fastest mile time. I will instead remember, first-timer Sara M. saying the word marathon during one of our early runs, getting a much needed popsicle from a little kid at a race, jumping on a trampoline with spectators on the Boston course, high fiving little kids and big kids on race courses, running alongside my first-timers from the start line to the finish line, joining in on the electric slide during the Boston marathon course, stopping in my tracks during the Marine Corps marathon when I came upon the "Blue Mile", running alongside my sister Debbie in the 1995 Chicago marathon, running alongside my brother Mike in the 2012 Boston marathon, giving and getting a FREE HUG from a race spectator, stopping mid race to have a donut with Allie while she was running her first marathon, running alongside Max in his first marathon and seeing him smile as bright and wide as a little kid at his own birthday party, doing a fun run with my friend Nicole that included a pit stop for ice cream cone. Every now and then we need to focus on our Experiences Per Hour and not just our miles per hour. The latter reflects our perseverance, determination and fight. The former brightens our soul.

On the Route—Variety is the spice of life, so add some spice to your runs by running a different route every now and then. Or, incorporate some of your to do list items into your run. Holy effectiveness, right? Some of my friends will use their training run to check out open houses. I have used my runs to hit up the post office for stamps or even meet my girlfriends for pizza by running straight to the restaurant. I had a client who had to do a lot of her long runs by herself. Instead of just extending her normal out and back route to get her mileage in, she would run point to point to a new destination. Then her family would pick her up at her finish spot. On the days that they were not available to pick her up, she would take the bus back home or a ride share. Another way to add variety to your training run, is to is to substitute a race for your run. Even if you have a 10-mile training run scheduled and you have a local 10K coming up, do some creative mileage and run an easy 4 miles before the race and then the race becomes the last 6 miles of your 10-miler. Just like that, the last 6 miles are supported, you have other people to run with and you even get a race shirt. I recommend getting in as much of the extra mileage in before the race because it might be mentally hard to restart running after you have crossed the finish line alongside everyone else. Mixing up your route is another great way to get through the miles. Join a fun run at your local running store for one of your midweek runs.

ABCs—Another trick of the trade that I use during my long runs and the latter miles of the marathon is the Gratitude Alphabet. This entails, naming people and experiences from my life that I am grateful for, for each letter of the alphabet. I can have more than one example for each letter. If I forget someone or an experience, I start all over at "A." If I get stuck on a letter, I also start over again at "A." This really came in handy in the fall of 2017, when I completed my first 100 miler. While I was out on the course for just under 27 hours, I actually went through the alphabet three times. In doing this, I came up with an additional step of naming "why" I am grateful for that person and/or experience. Before I knew it, the miles were clicking away. Not to mention, it's hard to be in a state of "Grrr" and a state of gratitude at the same time. During this same 100-miler, I also got through the miles by naming all of my teachers since pre-school. I went on to name all of my ex-boyfriends and good memories from each of them. Holy growth, right? I wanted to phone my therapist and let her know that I had truly moved on. You can also do other ABCs by naming cities, countries, car models, first names, authors, sports teams, etc. for each letter of the alphabet. If you get stuck on a letter start over.

Do It Yourself Playlist—When none of the above are working, try memorizing a song. I am dating myself here but it's still a great song. I memorized "*It Takes Two*" by DJ Rob Base on one of my long runs. I would play a little bit of the song and then replay it while I sang it. Once I had a section memorized, I started back at the beginning and played a little bit more of that song. I kept doing this until I was able to memorize the song. It's not pretty but it actually came in handy when I ran the Comrades marathon in Durban, South Africa. It was 56-mile race and we weren't allowed to wear headphones unless we wanted a big DQ (Disqualification).

Meet First-Timer, Christian B.

One word to describe my first marathon: Rollercoaster

Before my first marathon, the longest races I had run were 5Ks. I thought that those runs were going to be the most difficult miles ever; trust me, I was wrong! However, a scary and life changing event put me in the hospital and made me look at things differently. I had the urge do something challenging and rewarding. Around that same time, I met Coach Denise, who I like to call "The Original Running Gangster." Every time she came in to the chiropractic office I work in, she kept on "planting the "you can do it" marathon seed." Thanks to her continual encouragement, I finally found the courage to sign up. From the very beginning, before I even took a step, I just knew she believed in me and made me think I could do it. During training, every mile was new for me and after each run, I wanted out.

Throughout the process though, I realized if I really put my mind to something, I could accomplish it. It really hadn't occurred to me what was about to happen when I signed up. For example, I'd be worried I was going to get injured, but through the next run, I felt good. Or I thought I would be nervous for the race, but on race day, I was chill. I knew I was ready. On days when I thought I would quit, I would think about my nephew, Abad, who was born with a birth defect and would never be able to walk without braces. Even from a young age, he always worked to overcome his own obstacles. I felt like I was running for him. After finishing my first marathon, I thought I was "one and done." As time passed, that itch started to eat at me and I began to think about beating my time. I ran a second marathon and ended up improving by 30 minutes!

For other first-timers, I encourage you to believe that you can do it; people will start asking you about the training and suddenly you find yourself loving to talk about it. New runners should find a good running coach for their first marathon. It just makes the process easier - not that it's ever easy! Your long runs are where you find out what you can do—so don't skip out on them! And, of course, enjoy the ride. See you at the finish line!

If I could have a do over of my first marathon, I would make sure to run with a visor. The sun got really hot and it was blasting in my face during the latter miles.

Mile 12: Don't Be A T-Rex

Chapter focus: Zeroing in on proper running form.

In working with beginners, one of the first concerns that they have is that they do not know how to run. I am always surprised by this as running is just walking with a dose of "oomph", right? Think back to when you were little running on the playground. There was no thought about how to run or not run, you just ran. Running in adulthood is the same thing. For the most part, your running gait is driven by how your body is built and the strength and flexibility of your muscles. There are some key characteristics to be aware of for an effective running form, but for the most part, your body will "land" at its natural gait based on your own unique biomechanics. I know a lot of runners whose form looks like something is blatantly off, whether their right hip comes up more than the left or their head bobs to the right. Even a non-runner would think that something looks "off" with their running. Yet, these runners have qualified for Boston and some have even run sub 3:15 marathons. If you are still skeptical, go to the internet and search for videos of the female world record marathon (mixed gender- 2:15:25) holder, Paula Radcliffe. Aside from noticing her speed and effortlessness stride, you will also notice her head bobbing! A good litmus test to check your running form against is to compare your form to Phoebe in the *Friends* episode in which her and Rachel are running in Central Park. Make sure your form is nothing like Phoebe's.

Here are some key form mechanics to be conscious of when you are running:

1. "Hips to Nip"-When running, make sure that your arms are swinging alongside your body at a 90-degree angle. You want your arms to swing at this angle while rising up to your nipples and down to your hip, repeatedly. Think, "Hip to Nip"! You want your arms flowing freely alongside your body and not crisscrossing in front of your chest. By doing the latter, you are sending the momentum away from the forward plane that your body is creating. Where your movement goes, your energy will flow, so why send energy and momentum away from your body? Instead use that energy for momentum for moving forward. You want to make sure too, that your slightly clenched hands are not swinging directly in front of your arm pits resembling a T-Rex.

2. "Potato Chips"- While your arms are swinging effortlessly alongside your body, you want to make sure that your fists are not tightly clenched; visualize that you are carefully holding potato chips in your hand. If you instead clench your fists and crush the potato chips, the tenseness (or tension) in your hands will then drive up your arms through your neck and to your back. You want to be loose like *Mother Goose*!

3. "Mid Foot Strike"- With each foot strike, you want to make sure that your mid foot hits the ground first. You want to avoid running on your toes and your heels. Try running a few strides on your toes and then on your heels. Notice how awkward it feels? Boom! This is exactly why it doesn't feel natural or efficient to run on your toes or heels. One caveat

though is that when we sprint we naturally come up more on our toes.

4. "Shhh" - Run softly and carry a big hydration bottle, right? When your shoes contact the ground, you should not be able to hear them. You want to land softly. If you hear your shoes slapping the ground, this may be a sign that something is wrong with your gait. Note, however, in the latter miles of your marathon and/or your long runs, when our body and mind are tired, it is normal to hear your foot strike.

5. Don't try to lengthen your stride (i.e. over stride), as that can set you up for injury.

6. Stand tall, head up, shoulders back and relaxed. Imagine that there is a string pulling your head up.

If you are continually getting injured or you have a nagging injury that will not go away, you may benefit from getting an in-depth gait analysis from a licensed chiropractor, physical therapist or a podiatrist.

Meet First-Timer, Brenda C.

One word to describe my first marathon:
Emotional

Though I played sports in high school, I didn't really run unless I had to. That is until I saw my boyfriend go on runs and come home feeling amazing and full of energy. I downloaded a running app that motivated me to get running. That eventually lead me to running a women's half-marathon in New York City. When I finished the half, my friend and coach Denise, convinced me that I could also run a marathon. I figured "I survived the half - what is another 13.1 more miles?" It was a challenge and I love a good challenge. Denise believes in her runners. No matter if you are overweight or just starting to run. I never thought I would pick up running in my late 30's, but learning how to run has been rewarding. It's exciting when you can run a little bit longer each time without having to stop.

Training for a marathon is a part-time job and finding the time to run every other day can be challenging. I really think anyone can do a marathon but following the running plan is key. I wish I had been stricter with the training because I paid for every run that I missed on Marathon day. I had to travel a lot for work so I missed a lot of my training. 26.2 is a long distance and your body needs to be able to adapt to the miles.

The week of the marathon, I spent a lot of time looking up inspirational stories and advice for the day of the race. Race Day I was SO nervous! I got very emotional when I finished. I wanted to finish under the 6:30 time allowance but it took me 7:00:01. During the marathon, I told myself never again. I thought I was going to do one and be done, but a week later - when the pain went away - I was already thinking about improving my time.

If I could do my first marathon over, I would just be proud that I FINISHED a marathon and not be so down about my time. It's a huge accomplishment and I did it!

Mile 13: The Three Bears

Chapter Focus: How to prepare for a race that is too hot, too cold or just right!

Through running over 250 races across all climates and terrains, I have learned one certainty about race day. That certainty is the uncertainty of the weather. No matter how spot-on your training is, bad weather can adversely impact race day performance. As I mentioned in Mile 5, when dressing to run outdoors, you should add 20 degrees Fahrenheit to the outside temperature. This will minimize the chance of being too hot or too cold once you get into the groove of your run. From my experience, the most ideal temperature for race day is around 50 degrees Fahrenheit, wind and rain-free. Unless of course the wind is at your back. We will gladly welcome the wind at our back in any workout or race. In all of my marathons, I have probably only had 15 of them in ideal conditions.

Since we do not know what Mother Nature will bring us on race day, I recommend training in all types of weather with one caveat. That caveat is that you should not run in dangerous conditions. The more you power through training runs in "not so runner friendly" conditions, the easier race day will be for you mentally. For those races and runs that warrant too hot, too cold or too rainy conditions, I am here for you. I have competed in races in which "ma nature" gave me a run for my money, err medal so to speak. Though, if you do finish a race with crazy weather conditions, don that race shirt and medal with extra pride and bragging rights! In April 2018, I completed two extreme marathons in one week. I ran the Boston and London Marathons six days apart. Boston had 30-mile per hour winds and it rained the whole time. The weather didn't clear up until the next morning. London had the hottest temperatures on record. Now, if I see another runner with either race shirt on, I want to high five them because I know exactly what extra grit went into crossing each finish line!

A couple things to point out when we don't have favorable race day conditions. One is that you should thank the volunteers, spectators and police officers. They are selflessly supporting us and keeping us safe as we make our way to the finish line. Marathoning is our passion and it takes a village! We could not do it without them. Second, I remind myself when it's too hot, too cold and/or too rainy that I am not special. Everyone else that crosses the start line is going through the same non-runner-friendly weather. So, let's run on and cherish those race shirts with extra bragging rights.

The Year of the Sauna—The 2007 Chicago Marathon was one for the record books. This race was cancelled mid-stream as the temperatures soared to 88 degrees Fahrenheit. Even though I was primed to get a personal record that morning, I threw my time goal out the window. I instead set a goal of finishing safely without ending up in a medical tent. I had friends that did not run the race that day because the weather was so dangerously hot. My coach Greg, gave me really good advice marathon eve that I still adopt for hot races. I encourage you to do the same for your hot races. He recommended that any support crew that I have on the course have small bags of ice cubes available for me when I see them during the race. I know that his coaching, my cautious slower pace and this tip, contributed to me finishing the marathon before they canceled the race. I ran a 3:20:06 that year. I literally just ran "ice station" to "ice station." I would run with the bag of ice in one hand and loose ice cubes in the other. Going forward in hot marathons, I carry an empty bag to put ice in for me and for my clients. That marathon prepped me for the 2012 Boston Marathon, as the weather that year was also dangerously hot. It was so hot that the race organizers were letting you roll over your race registration to the following year. For both of these marathons, my mindset switched from *racing* the marathon to *running* the marathon.

For training runs in the heat, I recommend adapting your long run to be a short loop that you complete over and over. That way, when you start each loop, you can have access to a cooler with frozen water bottles or ice cubes. You can also run a short loop that has a convenience store on the loop. That way, you can hydrate, refuel and even take care of the "plumbing" on each loop. I also recommend running in the early morning or at dusk. Another option is to move your run indoors when it is hot and/or humid out or to a cooler day later in the week. As mentioned in Mile 5, make sure too, that you are running in light colored, breathable clothing.

Stormy Weather—In all of my marathons, I have only had three that I had to run in the rain. The 2007 & 2018 Boston and the 2013 Nashville marathons. The 2018 Boston, was the first marathon that I have run that was 95 percent mental and 5 percent physical! Having only run three rainy marathons, I am still learning how to dress properly. Through trial and error though, I have swum away, so to speak, with useful insight that you can now apply to your rainy marathon(s). Below are some of my tricks of the trade for marathoning in the rain:

1. Make sure that you have a water-proof jacket. Water repellent will not cut it.

2. Apply more than your usual amount chafing products to your chafe prone areas. Especially your feet.

3. I ran in Balega® mohair socks for the first time at the 2018 Boston Marathon and I did not get one blister. I also did not bruise one toe nail. The latter was a first! It turns out, mohair

is great in all temperatures because it regulates to your body temperature.

4. If you can, wear an old pair of running shoes to the start line and have the shoes that you will run in enclosed in a sealable bag. Pack a dry pair of socks to put on when you put your race shoes on.

5. If you don't have a water proof jacket, wear a rain poncho or a garbage bag to help keep you dry and warm.

6. If you run with your phone, make sure to have it enclosed in a sealable bag. I actually double bag my phone.

7. In the 2007 Boston marathon, we kept our toes dry by having duct tape wrapped around the toe box of each shoe. This helped minimize blisters

8. Pack dry clothes and shoes for post-race in a sealable bag. Flip flops are great for post-race too.

9. Before heading out the door, tie grocery bags around your shoes to help keep the rain out.

10. If it is warm enough weather, wear supportive flip flops until it is time to put your race shoes on.

11. If it is cold and rainy, wear merino wool as the layer closest to your skin to help keep you warm and dry.

12. In your training, practice running in the rain even if it's only a couple of miles. This will help you figure out what gear will actually keep you dry and blister free.

The Most Beautiful Place on Earth—Having survived over 2 decades of Chicago winter running and the 2008 Antarctica Marathon, I have also accumulated tricks of the trade with how to dress in cold weather. First off, did I mention that Antarctica is the most beautiful place that I have ever been to? I was plenty prepared for running that marathon because of my experience running on the Chicago Lakefront in the winter. For the most part, you want to do what you can to keep your hands, feet and ears warm. Once one of these body parts gets cold, you might as well throw in the snow shovel.

1. Choose mittens over gloves! I learned this from Coach Greg in that your hands will stay warmer when your fingers are all together in mittens rather than separated within gloves. It's the skin on skin effect. I actually take it a step further and wear what I call, "glittens". They are gloves that have a mitten cover. Depending upon the weather, you can transform the glitten into gloves or mittens. For the latter option, I stuff hand warmers in the glitten when it's really cold out. I swear by my hand warmer and glitten combo!

2. Merino wool should be the closest material to your skin. This will help keep your body heat in and absorb the sweat so that your core stays warm and dry. I wore merino wool when I ran the Antarctica and Reykjavik marathons. I also wore Icebreaker merino wool during my 100-mile run where the overnight temperature dropped to 22 degrees Fahrenheit. Some clothing manufacturers make different weights of merino wool which help with layering. Once you have the merino wool layer as your base layer, you can then layer it with a warm, breathable, wind resistant jacket. For milder temperature runs, I recommend a merino wool long sleeved top coupled with a breathable vest.

3. Cover your Noggin! Just a word of caution when you are selecting a winter running hat. I recommend that you double, triple check the fitting of your hat by running back and forth in the store with the hat on. That way you will be able to tell if that hat will stay in place and actually keep your ears covered when you run. I have had to give away so many cute winter hats because the hat would ride up over my ears once I started running with it. In selecting the right hat, also make sure that it will keep you warm, while also wick away your sweat.

4. Speed with Caution-During the cold and black ice laden Chicago winters, I move most of my speed workouts to the treadmill or even the stairwell. For me it›s not worth wiping out on black ice, getting injured and then having to rehab in the spring instead of train. Proceed with caution, my friends! Also, if you can, choose dry pavement over trails or snowy sidewalks. This should help minimize your wipe-outs.

You are 1 in 400 Trillion—Regardless of whether the weather is mild or extreme, you should always listen to your body. If you are feeling faint, light headed, dizzy, etc. during a race or run, please seek medical attention. It is not worth risking your life for a finish line. Races are a dime a dozen, while you on the other hand are 1 in 400 trillion! Personally, I quit a swim during my 3rd Ironman triathlon. I was about 45 minutes into the 2.4-mile swim, when I just could not get my heart rate down. I reminded myself that I had already completed this race distance twice before and that I had put in the training to finish. Heck, I was even trying to distract my fear by telling myself how beautiful the tree-lined Russian River was that I was swimming in. To no avail, I still could not relax. I was the last athlete in the water but then the competitors from the shorter distance races started swimming alongside me and on top of the water therefore churning up the water. I was freaked out, to say the least. I knew that that day was not my day for racing. I then calmly waved for a lifeguard to get me out of the water. As a coach, I initially had my tail between my legs in embarrassment. I thought, "What kind of coach quits a race?" Then I realized, I was practicing what I preach by quitting when my mind was no longer in the game and I was putting my life at risk.

Meet First-Timer, Padraic K.

One word to describe my first marathon:
Transformative

I ran cross-country in high school but before training for the marathon, I hadn't run more than a 5K in over ten years. My wife signed up for the Chicago Triathlon to raise money for Cystic Fibrosis (CF), which took our friend's life when she was 19 years old. I thought this was an overly ambitious idea, but I started training with her and was enjoying how it made me feel to exercise so much. I decided I wanted to have an end goal too, so I signed up for the Chicago Marathon. I also fundraised for CF. Together, we completed our physical challenges and ended up raising over $3,000. The night after the marathon, I wasn't sure I'd do another. The week after, I was sure. Now, I'm looking forward to my next one.

Even for beginners, training for a marathon is surprisingly manageable if you do it correctly, with enough time and focus. Training for a marathon isn't a sprint, it's a marathon. Little by little, you start to do things that you once thought were impossible and that is an addicting feeling. The human body, including yours, can do amazing things. I met inspiring person after inspiring person, of all ages and backgrounds. Your body, mind, and diet will all change for the better. Also, every part of your day contributes to your run performance and every part of your body is connected in amazing ways that contributes to your running form and performance, too.

I learned it's never too late to start something big. I met many runners, even on race day, who said they had a desk job for 20 years and then started running. That changed my perspective about running completely. I learned that running, which looks like such a solo sport to an outsider, is nothing without the community that is behind it all. Find a support group for your training and it will change your life for the better.

One thing that I learned on race day that I wish that I knew beforehand was that nipple chafing is not a joke - it can get so bad it will make you want to stop; prepare properly.

Mile 14: What the Hill?

Chapter focus: How to creatively train for specificity when you don't have exact race day terrain.

One of the key principles of marathon training is the concept of *specificity*. In layman's terms, this means, if you want to run a marathon you have to practice running and run a lot. It would not benefit you on race day, if you trained for your marathon by solely playing golf or shooting pool, etc. Also, it would not benefit you on marathon morning if you only ran short distances in your training. In order words, to best prepare for race day, you want to train for the skill(s) and conditions that you will face on race day. For instance, if you live in the flat lands of Chicago like me and you are running the Big Sur or Boston marathon, you will need to incorporate hills into your training to best prepare for race day. Another example is if you are running the New York or Boston marathon. Since these races start in the late morning, you will want to run your long run later in the morning and not first thing. This will help mimic what race day will be like and therefore help you fine tune the timing and the type of nutrition you will have for race eve dinner and on race day.

I first learned about specificity when I was training for my first Ironman triathlon. At first, I could not understand why my coach recommended that I save my long runs for the evening time instead of early in the morning. His reasoning was that by running in the early evening, I was able to practice the timing and type of nutrition I would use on race day as well as get my body acclimated to running in the warm evening temperatures instead of cooler pre-dawn temperatures. He also had me do my long ride the day before my long run as this would be the order I would be riding and running on race day. He wanted me to practice running long miles on already tired legs.

I recommend if you are doing a race outside of your hometown that you do your due diligence to get an understanding of what the terrain will be like, as well as the likely race day temperature. That way, you can modify your training if you need to. Some marathons provide a course tour in which you drive the actual course. Seeing the course ahead of time can help you with visualizing your race and having a better idea of what to expect race day. A lot of marathons also provide a topography map of the course. For me, I have to physically feel the course with each foot strike in order to know the impact of the terrain versus viewing a map or riding the course. What I have found helpful though is comparing topography maps to marathons that I have run. There are also race portals and blogs that you can use to research your race. A couple of sites you can use for reviews and research are raceraves.com and bibbz.net.

Do It Yourself Hills—So, how exactly does a flat lander train for hills outside of treadmilling on an incline? In training for a hilly marathon, I use the following man-made substitutes for Mother Nature-made hills. My go-to is stairwells. When I first started doing stairs, I would climb for 15 minutes twice a week. Once 15 minutes became manageable, I then climbed for 30 minutes twice a week. I do not run up or down the stairs as it will increase the probability that I will trip. I initially started with climbing one step at a time. Once I was able to climb for 45 minutes, I then started climbing every other step. This is the closest I want to get to "running" stairs. Through practice and consistency, I am now able to do 2 hours of stairs in one workout. The stairs are a trifecta workout. They replicate squats, lunges and a speed workout all in one. It is a very effective use of my limited time. To help pass the steps, I listen to podcasts or an e-book. Another man-made hill option, which is what we used to do to prepare for Boston in the 1990s, is to run parking garage ramps early in the morning before they get crowded.

You can of course use a stair climber and treadmill at the gym but I feel like I am at least moving forward with my two options above. If you did not have access to either of these machines or you were unable to get in these types of workouts, don't sweat it. Just walk the hills! From my own experience doing hilly races without proper hill training, I have learned that it is better to just walk the hills instead of trying to run them. What I have found, is that the pace I "run" the hill and "walk" the hill is almost the same. By walking the hill though, I don't burn out my quads. Now, whenever I see hills, I no longer cringe or curse them. I instead embrace the hill because it's walking time!

Running Strong On Tired legs—No matter the distance of the race, I believe that it is during the last 20-25 percent of the race when the race actually starts. It is at this point in the race, in which your legs no longer have a spring in their step. You now have to call upon mental strength more so then physical strength to power through to the finish. Just like most kids have selective hearing, so do your legs. They are selectively listening to your brain. They are moving, but not at the pace you want them to move—they feel as if they are made of concrete. To minimize concrete legs, I recommend the following specificity workouts to help make your legs run strong even when they are tired:

1. After your long runs, run 4 to 6 quarter mile repeats with 3-4 minutes of passive rest.
2. If you cross train with cycling (indoor or outdoor), run 15 to 30 minutes after your ride.
3. After climbing stairs, run 15 to 30 minutes afterwards.

Before adding these types of workouts, however, make sure that you already have a strong running base. The first few times that you do these workouts, they will seem hard but your body will adapt and they will get easier because you will get stronger. Come race day, your legs will be more in sync with your brain and they will fly instead of fight during that last 25 percent.

Meet First-Timer, Sara M.

One word to describe my first marathon:
Empowering

Before my first marathon, I had been running
for several years off and on. I always enjoyed
participating in sport teams during high school
but in my twenties, I really just limited my fitness
to classes at the gym or jogging on my own at a comfortable pace. I have
always been heavy and never imagined running any races because I thought
running races was only for skinny fitness folk. A group that I didn't fit in
with. I hired Denise as my running coach honestly to help motivate me to
consistently keep up with my running and help me drop some weight—in
the end, she opened my eyes to a really wide community that is quite diverse.

People of all shapes and sizes run marathons - something Denise taught me.
Your body is capable of accomplishing incredible things including running
a marathon as long as you put in the time to train properly. The training
helps you avoid injuries. In the words of Denise, "With a little 'RunSpiration'
anything is possible!" During our runs, Denise would distract me by sharing
tales of her RaceCations around the world. After hearing her constantly
ask me about participating in a marathon, I relented and we ran the Paris
Marathon together. I had a secondary goal of giving my mother the medal
for her birthday. I think setting fitness goals are important in a weight loss
journey because it distracts from having a constant focus on the scale. I
learned that my mind and body are stronger then I imagined. The race was
definitely a challenge - the last 5 miles were really a test of my personal limits
mentally and physically.

I thought I would complete one marathon and that would be it. I was wrong!
I am currently signed up for my hometown marathon this year. It will be the
ultimate joy to run my first marathon in the US in the beautiful city that holds
a special place in my heart: Chicago!

If I could have a do over of my first marathon, I would make sure that I had a
new playlist to run to and not the same one from my training season. I didn't
have new music and it was tricky getting my mind to relax.

Mile 15: Treat Yo' Self

Chapter focus: How to stay motivated run in and run out

Every now and then you will have those days that you just don't want to do your homework. Running will be the last thing you want to do. A lot of my first-timers will start running out of steam around six to eight weeks into the season. This lack of motivation is even worse in the latter weeks as you start getting mentally and physically burnt out. Not to worry, as this is a normal reaction. Twenty weeks is a long semester especially when you have other accountabilities outside of training. Marathoning is a huge sacrifice. You sacrifice hard-earned cash on the registration fee. You sacrifice your discretionary free time to train. If you run long on the weekend, you more than likely sacrifice Friday or Saturday nights to ensure that you are ready to go on long run morning. The macro reward for all of this though will come at the finish line. You will not just receive a finisher's shirt and a medal but more importantly a huge sense of accomplishment and self-pride. The reward will definitely be worth the sacrifice.

I believe that you should also have micro rewards throughout your training. These will help you when your motivation tank is depleted. This is where my Denise-hack of sacrifice and reward comes into play. Let's just say the voice in your head is telling you to, "just say no" to your workout.

To change that voice to, "just say go," I recommend you give yourself a reward for go, go, going. The reward doesn't have to be anything grandiose, although I do encourage grandiose rewarding when you visit the Marathon Expo. A reward can be whatever you want: post run donut (my favorite), wireless head phones, pizza (my other favorite), running gear, audio book on your wish list, concert tickets, pedicure, post long run nap, massage, all of the above, etc. Some of my runners have even gotten a 26.2 tattoo after their first marathon. I have a lot of friends and family who are all about reward, reward, reward. To me, putting some muscle tears in the game, makes my rewards that much more valuable when I partake in them.

Whenever I participate in a marathon, 100-miler or a Ironman triathlon, I will treat myself to something I normally would not. That way, when I use or see that reward down the road, it will spark memories from that race and in turn have more weight to it because I earned it. I didn't just buy it. For instance, when I ran the Honolulu Marathon, I bought a knit cap at a surf shop that looks like an ice cream cone. I grabbed it on our first day of vacation and put it back on the shelf. I then decided during the marathon that the hat would be my marathon reward. It's one of my favorite hats, not just because it's fun but also because I know what extra fight went into it. When I completed the 2003 Wisconsin Ironman triathlon, I rewarded myself with a trip to Kona, Hawaii a month later to see the World Championship Ironman competition. Now that is a reward, right? Even our race shirts have more weight in them then a singlet we just pulled off a shelf.

In order to stay motivated season to season, I will sign up for a destination race(s). Since swimming and biking are not my first and second choice for working out, I signed up for a destination triathlon to keep me motivated to cross train and not just run all the time. Training for this triathlon was the sacrifice and the reward was competing in the race in wine country and then the post-race celebrating in the area with my friends. I also bought some pretty awesome swag at the race expo as additional rewards. Having a destination to look forward to visiting and racing in keeps me motivated to put the training in. Check out Mile 23 for some great destination race ideas.

Meet First-Timer, Andy L.

One word to describe my first marathon: Unforgettable

Before signing up to train for the 2017 Nashville Rock & Roll Marathon, I had only done a few smaller distance races. I started running regularly in the spring of 2016. The last time I had trained for any type of distance was back in high school. Once I got back into a training routine, I was hooked. After finishing my first 5k in 2016, I loved the feeling of accomplishment. I decided to continue to run because I wanted to challenge myself. I was inspired to run a full marathon after successfully completing a 5K and a half-marathon. Doubling my distance felt like the next logical step—I felt that runner's high and I needed to get on to the next challenge.

Throughout my training and finally at race day, I learned that the sport of running is somewhat an extension of my personality. By that, I mean I never give up and can be steadfastly stubborn. Especially when it comes to finishing anything that I start. A marathon is a challenge that I think many people are up for because in my experience, running is three-quarters a mental challenge. The physical part is tolerable once you get past any ideas, thoughts or doubts standing in your way. When I signed up for the marathon, I already knew that I wanted to run one again. I wanted to take advantage of my training and continue to rise to new challenges. In fact, over the course of the following year, I ran three more marathons!

If I could have a do over of my first marathon, I would make sure that I get to the race on time.

Mile 16: Jack be Limber, Jack can be Quick

Chapter focus: The importance of incorporating dynamic and static stretching into your training regimen to help prevent injury.

Stretching Does the Body Good

Has any topic in running been debated at such length? Should you stretch, or shouldn't you? Before your run or after? Bounce or no bounce? The two types of stretches that we will be discussing here are dynamic and static. With dynamic stretching, you are repeatedly moving your joints and muscles through a full range of motion. These are done to get your heart rate going and to get your joints and muscles loosened up before you start your run. Basically, they are a wakeup call for your muscles and your nervous system. A dynamic warm-up is important for increasing blood flow to the muscles and priming the nervous system for the work that's about to be done. With static stretching, you hold the muscle stretch in place. These types of stretches are done to increase your flexibility. Many studies have concluded that dynamic stretching combined with a short warm up beforehand and static stretching after your run is beneficial to performance and preventing injury.

In regards to stretching, here are some high-level do's and don'ts:

- To continue to drive this important point home, dynamic stretches should be done before running and static stretches should follow your run.

- Do stretch with each workout and even on your off days.

- Do breathe deeply with each stretch. You should notice that you are able to stretch further on your last stretch then the first stretch in a series.

- Do not stretch past the point of pain. You should just stretch to the point of a minor amount of tension.

- Just like there is no bouncing in baseball, there is no bouncing in stretching. Bouncing causes micro tears in your muscles. Tears create scar tissue, which makes you less flexible and can cause pain.

- Yoga is a great compliment to static stretching.

I have included examples of dynamic and static stretches in Aid Station 2.

Meet First-Timer, Gordana S.

One word to describe my first marathon: Fun

Running was never my sport because I never thought that I could do it. Growing up I hated to run. Ironically, I was always one of those people that just watched runners from the side and dreamed of becoming one. In my adulthood, I wanted to try but I always thought I would fail, so I had no courage or motivation to begin.

A close friend of mine was a runner who consistently ran twice a week. I would always say to her that I wish I could run—even if it's only 3 miles. With that friend as inspiration, I decided to get professional help and met Coach Denise. I was so nervous of what she would think of me and my running, I also have to admit I was embarrassed. Right away, Coach Denise made me feel very comfortable and made me realize that it could be done. We started off slowly and kept adding on miles to every run! I was in heaven every time I hit a new longer distance!!! It's a feeling I can't describe. When we initially started working together, my goal was to run a half- marathon. She helped me train and even ran it with me! Shortly after, she encouraged me to sign up for my first full marathon! Oh my gosh, at that time what was I thinking, "Me? Running 26.2 miles?" Though I had trained, I still thought I was crazy for taking on this challenge. My first marathon was worth it though and I am already signed up for my fourth marathon. I just wish I had met Denise much earlier in my life but still thankful that I did!

Through my training process, I realized that anything is possible. If you set your mind to achieve something that you once thought was impossible, think again: "It's possible." After that, all you need is hard work, commitment and dedication. If I did it, you can too! It's the best feeling crossing that finish line knowing that you just did it. You want all the world to know.

On race day, I really learned how much the spectators help by cheering you on. I never really hit the wall in my marathon because of them.

Mile 17: RunSpiration

Chapter focus: How to get inspired and inspire others throughout this RunVenture.

What do you do when you feel like your "Oomph" tank is nearing empty but you still have 10 more miles left to your run? Or worse, you are only 4 weeks into the training season and you are losing the motivation to get out the door? You look for RunSpiration.

Throughout my running career, I have drawn inspiration from within and from others around me. When I am losing my fight and want to quit, I remind myself how bad I want it. I think of my end goal. I think of other things that didn't come easy to me but I pushed through and gave 110 percent to achieve it. I visualize my old coach cheering me on at races. Speaking of race day cheerleaders, I cannot help but have extra spring in my step seeing complete strangers on the sidelines cheering us on. Here they are helping us do what we love, when we don't even know each other's names. When I hit my mental wall in a race, one of my go-tos to help with plowing ahead is to visualize each of my clients. Day in and day out, I get to take a passenger seat to this raw human inspiration. The look on their faces when they are fighting through a workout and then completing it is what replenishes that lost oomph.

Monkey See, Monkey Can Also Do—I mentioned in my introduction that the reason I ever thought I could do a marathon is because my sister, Debbie, ran one and showed me that a marathon was no longer super-human. It was humanly possible and better yet, within reach. I confess, there is a hidden agenda behind me including stories of my first-timers in this book. That agenda is that I am hoping you will relate to one of the first-timers, that one of them will do for you what my sister did for me.

Following a similar agenda, I encourage my new runners and marathon naysayers to volunteer at a marathon. Most impactful and powerful is volunteering at the finish line where they can hand out the medals. That way, they see people of every age, size and pace out there doing something that they may also think is a super-human feat. I encourage you to get the future marathoners in your circle to do the same. Start planting the marathon seed with them and have them volunteer at your marathon. An indirect benefit of each of us out there marathoning is that you never know what spectator, volunteer, or even police officer we will inspire. Boom! Monkey see, monkey can also do!

Raw Human Inspiration—Whenever I meet a first-timer who is beyond overwhelmed about their marathon or when I meet a future first-timer who uses the word marathon in their vocabulary but hasn't hit the submit button yet, I direct them to two of my favorite marathon documentaries. One is Jon Dunham's *"Spirit of the Marathon"* and the other is *"PBS's Nova Documentary, Boston Marathon Challenge."* Both from 2007, these documentaries highlight everyday people and their marathon journey. I own both of these documentaries. I know how they start and how they end, yet, I still get inspired and am brought to proud tears when I see each runner cross the finish line. That finish line changes us! If and when you feel a little angst about your marathon, I encourage you to watch both of these documentaries at the start of the season and then again marathon weekend. BTW, that's one of my mentors, Coach Megerle from Tufts in the PBS documentary!

Remember Your "Why"—On those days that you just don't want to get out the door and even during the marathon when you are running out of steam, I want you to revisit your Why. Your Why is what inspired you to hit "submit" on the race website. To choose training runs over time with your non-running friends & family. To choose an early Saturday morning run over a late Friday night with your peeps or family. Some of you may even have a why outside of yourself; raising awareness and funds for a charity near and dear to your heart.

Our Whys are powerful and will earn their weight in gold come race day. Throughout my marathon career, my Whys have changed. When I initially started marathoning, my Why was all about proving to myself and to others that I could do it and that I could get faster and faster. I was using my finish times as a way to validate my worth. This is a whole separate book. After my accident, my Why instead focused on gratitude. Gratitude to even be able to run, let alone marathon. Now, my Why drives me to help runners achieve their marathon goals while having fun along the way. For additional proof on how strong our Whys can be, think of other things that you have done in your life before that you wanted so badly and you had to work so hard to get through. Your Why at that time fueled your achievement and commitment.

Marathon Mantras—When I am actually racing a marathon, there comes a time when I want to quit and I question why I signed up. Yes, not every marathon I run is filled with unicorns and rainbows. About 90 percent are! For those 10 percent that aren't, I call on some of my mantras to help me power through. This helps change the current, "I can't do this," "this sucks!" station in my head to the "you can and you will do it!" station. Try some of my mantras out or come up with your own in your training runs. You can then call upon them in your marathon to help you close the deal and ward off any not so positive stations streaming race day. Here are some of my go-to mantras:

- "Embrace the Suck"
- "I am Stronger Then the Suck"
- "Fight! Fly!"
- "The Hurt Means I am Alive"
- "Stay in the Game, Don't Quit"
- "This Will Pass"
- "I Can and I Will"

Meet First-Timer, Darryl E.

One word to describe my first marathon:
Inspiring

Before signing up for the marathon, I had a long but apathetic relationship with running. In high school, I trained and ran for the cross-country team. However, after organized sports were over, twenty years passed where I hardly ran or exercised at all. When I celebrated my thirty-ninth birthday, I decided it was time to get in shape. I began running daily and really took to the routine - I just didn't stop. I got in a groove where I was running between three and five miles a day and getting out there six days a week. It felt good, but I never pushed myself further and fell into a comfortable rhythm that became a kind of rut. Thinking it was an insurmountable task, I put off the idea of running a marathon. Finally, though, I thought to myself, "if not now, never," and took the plunge to sign up. After my first marathon, I think about running another all the time—I've caught the bug—but life events that have taken up that time have prevented it. I haven't run another one…yet.

Throughout my training, my wife was my inspiration. She supported me and then became my example as well. She ran her first marathon less than a year after our third child was born. I know people "think" they can't run a marathon, but I really believe anyone can do it. The challenge is all about where your head is at—as it is 99% mental.

If I could have a do over of my first marathon, I would not go out as fast. I suffered during the last few miles as a result.

Mile 18: The Long Run—
Your Weekly Quiz

Chapter focus: How your long runs help you fine tune your race day gear, nutrition and pacing strategy.

Each week of your training, you will have one long run on your plate. As I mentioned in Mile 4, if you have to miss any workouts during the week, you want to make sure that you do not miss this run. Completing as many of the long runs as you can, will build not just your physical endurance but also your mental endurance for race day. They will also help you fine tune the nutrition and pacing that will work and not work come marathon morning. Once your long runs start getting over two hours, they become the most critical runs of your training next to your 20-mile training run. Think of these workouts as your weekly take home quizzes!

Testing 1, 2, 3, 4—In preparing for your long runs, minimize working your legs the day before. You want your legs to be rested and ready to seize the miles! The night before your long run, it's a good idea to practice the timing and content of your nutrition. Figuring out the perfect combination of what you eat and when, helps to figure out marathon morning "plumbing", if you know what I mean. The last thing that you want to do during a race is to stop to use a bathroom. These "plumbing" stops don't just break your race day mojo but they also take up clock time. It only took one marathon eve dinner of Penne Arrabbiata for me to learn the hard way that there was too much spice in my life. The next morning, I set a personal record in the number of bathroom stops during a marathon. If only this was an honor! Your long runs should be run at conversation pace. Either try to run the same pace throughout the run or else run a negative split for the run. The latter is when you run the second half of the run faster than the first half. Either of these approaches are recommended for race day. I am a big fan of negative splitting. I find it easier to pace around a first half and second half then pace every single mile. Plus, it's better to have some extra spring in your step in those latter miles when your mind isn't as positive as the early, fun miles. These runs are also a great opportunity to test out your gear. Use these long runs to practice for the Big Day!

Throughout each long run, you are not just *physically* conditioning your body to handle 26.2 miles but you are also *mentally* conditioning your mind to handle 26.2. All of this practice will then transition to race weekend! Depending upon your running background, your long runs will start at 3 to 6-miles a pop and then increase about 10 percent each week. Staying close to this 10 percent will help to minimize injuries. For three weeks in a row, we will build up the long run distance and then the 4th week is considered a cut back week. For these long runs, we bring the mileage down to give your body and mind a break. Then, we get right back at it and build up another 3 weeks in a row until we get you to the big Kahuna: the 20-miler. To get through your long runs, it helps to run with a group or a training partner, especially when the mileage is in the double digits. Then, post run, you can all reward together. Mmm, pancakes! Not to mention, there is strength in numbers. When I used to run with my group, I found that there were days when I was having a hard time getting through the run and my running peeps would pull me through. There were also days when some of my running peeps were having a hard time and I would help get them through the run. Another option to help you log those long runs is to find a local race and use it for a majority of your mileage. You can either add the additional mileage before the race or after the race. From my experience though, it's better to run the extra mileage before the race because once you cross the finish line, it's sometimes hard to restart.

Creative Long Running—If life gets in the way and you cannot get your long run in, you can do a modified long run. One option to modify your long run is to break up your long run into two runs in the same day, i.e. "two-a-day." I recommend that you run at least 70 percent of the total long run distance in the first run because you want to take advantage of time on your feet and run a distance that is further than your weekday runs. A second option with creative long running is to split up the mileage between two back to back days. Again, I recommend that at least 70 percent of your long run total mileage is completed in the first run. With both of these options you still get the distance in, you just get the benefit of recovery time that you would not normally get if you did your long run in one shot.

Meet First-Timer, Natalie R.

One word to describe my first marathon:
Monumental

I was always a very active person and played volleyball and basketball, but I used to cringe at the thought of running longer than a single mile. Even after being asked several times, I never signed up for my high school track team because the warm up was 2 miles...yeah, nope. I caught the running bug after my first 3.5-mile race at my company's corporate challenge. That race was the furthest I'd run at that point. It was my friend Abby who inspired me to take it further. She started asking me to join her for short distances here and there. I signed up for a 5K, 10K and a half-marathon. I was amazed I could run 13.1, but never dreamed I would actually do a full marathon. One year after my first half-marathon, and after a few drinks, Abby and I agreed to run a marathon! I didn't look back after that.

Right before my first marathon I told Coach Denise, "This will be my only one. I just want to cross it off the bucket list and see if I can do it." Boy, was I wrong. Fast forward to my second marathon, where I shaved off 64 minutes from my first marathon time, finishing with a 4:14. What an emotional and fulfilling experience. I will come back for more. I owe a lot of my success as well to my running coach and friend, Denise. She provided me with important skills for training and race day during our weekly track workouts and she even paced me during my second marathon.

You'd be extremely surprised what your body is capable of. Yes, it is physically and mentally grueling at times -- but I promise you: the end result is worth EVERY BIT. Stressful situations don't seem so stressful anymore. There is no such thing as limitations if you put your mind to something. I learned and continue to learn through my race training, that You. Can. Do. Anything. It's true. The power of positive thinking is HUGE. Think you can and you will. Visualize you can and you will. Through hours of training and being alone with my thoughts, this concept has finally sunk in and I believe it now. Let's just say, it hasn't always been that way and I devote a lot of my self-growth to running.

One thing that I learned on race day that I wish I knew beforehand, was -
NEVER wear new clothing on race day. During my first marathon, I mistakenly
wore a new sports bra and boy did I pay for it. After multiple bandage dressings
and 3 weeks of healing, I was back to normal.

Mile 19: Got Speed?

Chapter Focus: How to get faster by incorporating speed workouts into your training.

This happened to me and it happens to a majority of my first-timers. Throughout the training and during our marathon, we tell ourselves that we are only going to do one marathon. If I had a pizza for every time I heard this, I could have free pizza for life. Heck, I didn't even know if I could finish one, let alone think about a second or 100th marathon. From my unofficial polling of first-time marathoners since 1994, I guesstimate that 10 percent of first- time marathoners hold true to being "one and done." So, what happens to the other 90 percent of us? Having completed the "no longer intimidating" marathon and having something magical ignite inside of us, we realize that wasn't so bad after all. We want to marathon again, only this time around, we want to run faster. My first marathon was so long ago that I don't remember how much time had to pass before my famous last words of "never again" changed to "where can I sign up?" This mile is for those of you that are also with me in that 90 percent.

I ran three more marathons on my own and my times barely improved.

If you looked up insanity in the dictionary at the time, it would have been a picture of me with a look of frustration and exhaustion. I was training the same way over and over and not understanding why I wasn't racing faster. I decided that I needed to break my own insanity and do things differently. I brought in the big guns because I didn't want to just get faster, I wanted to qualify for Boston! I met a girl who had qualified for Boston at her first marathon. I asked her how she did it. She shared with me that she got faster from doing track workouts. She invited me to her coach's workouts. My first month or two of reactions were, "No Thank You!" or "Running on a track is like high school gym class" and "I hated running in gym class." Fast forward to June 1998 when I finally caved and joined her and my new coach Greg for weekly track workouts. One season with Greg and I qualified for Boston!

Gritervals—What I have learned from training with Greg and from coaching my clients is that you don't know how much faster you can be, until you start adding consistent speed workouts to your training. Even if you weren't fast in high school, let alone a runner until you picked up this book, it doesn't mean that you can't be fast. Before sharing how to run track workouts, I want to first explain what a track workout entails. In running track workouts, you run short intervals at fast speeds with rest in between each interval. An interval can also be called a repeat. By incorporating these types of workouts into your training, you will see your paces improve. An interval can be as short as a 50-yard dash and even as long as 3 miles. I call intervals "gritervals" because unlike most of our conversation paced mileage, getting through intervals requires extra grit. Hence, the term griterval. Since this is a harder workout than an easy run, I recommend that you don't run an interval workout close to a long run. When you first start gritervalling, I recommend that you start with 1 mile in total of gritervals. This can be 1 mile fast, 4 separate quarter miles or even 2 separate half miles. Then, every 3 weeks, you add an additional half mile of gritervals. If you start gritervalling at the beginning of your marathon training, this will build up to 4 miles of total gritervalling in your 20-week season.

Here are a couple examples of Griterval workouts

Griterval Workout A:

- Run a quarter of a mile at "Need Oxygen" pace. (see Mile 8 for pacing)
- Rest in place for 3-4 minutes.
- Run a quarter of a mile at "Need Oxygen" pace.
- Rest in place for 3-4 minutes.
- Run a quarter of a mile at "Need Oxygen" pace.
- Rest in place for 3-4 minutes.
- Run a quarter of a mile at "Need Oxygen" pace.

Griterval Workout B:

- Run a half of a mile at "Need Oxygen" pace.
- Rest in place for 3-4 minutes.
- Run a half of a mile at "Need Oxygen" pace.

Consistency is Key—In order to see results with gritervals, you need to be consistent. First, you need consistency *of* the workout. You need to do intervals at least once or twice a week in order to see results. If you do one griterval workout a month, it will take you a lot longer to see your paces improve. Second, you also want to be consistent *within* a workout. What this means is that you want all of your gritervals in a workout to be around the same pace. For instance, in Workout A above, you don't want to go all out on the first quarter-mile and bonk on the other three quarter-miles. You also do you want to sand bag the last quarter, while floating through the first three. Instead, aim to run all four of them around the same pace. This is similar to how you want to race. When you race, you don't want to go all out in the early miles and you don't want to go so slow that you sand bag to the last miles. Instead you want to go a pace that comfortable challenges you, yet you can hold for pretty much the whole time. Again, this is if you are racing a race and not running a race.

Your gritervals will be at "need oxygen" pace or slower, depending upon the distance. At a minimum, you need to run your gritervals faster than your go-to conversation pace. The shorter the griterval distance, the less you should be able to talk during it. On the contrary, the longer the griterval, the more you should be able to talk but not want to because it's still hard to talk. My talk test for pacing is covered more in Mile 8.

My last consistency principle is that the more you can keep up with your speed, season to season, the more each griterval season will build upon the next season. A lot of my clients will do speed workouts with me for their marathon season. Once they run their marathon, they do not do speed again until the following year's marathon season starts up again. What frustrates them is that the pace they end the season at is no longer the same as the pace they are starting the next season at. I worked with my coach for eleven years and ran speed workouts year-round. The first year that I ran with him, my marathon time was 3:37. In my ninth year working with Greg, my marathon time dropped to a 3:15.

Two additional tips about gritervals is that, one you can always substitute a 5K race for a griterval workout provided you are racing the 5K and not running it. Secondly, when you run each griterval, try not to go over the designated rest period, as doing so counteracts the hard work that you just put your body and mind through.

Taxation Does the Body Good—When I first started running track workouts, there was a girl in our group who would lap me, all while exhaling obnoxiously. She was a former collegiate runner. She would lap me on the track and I would think, "why is she breathing so heavy, shouldn't she slow down?" When I ran our track workouts, I don't remember breathing that loudly and taxed. Then, I realized that the more mileage I ran at a taxed breathing pace, the more my paces improved. Eventually, I started passing her in our track workouts and even at races. Damn, if my high school cross country coach could see me now. When I run intervals now, my breathing is very taxed but controlled. No matter the distance of the interval, try to run them at a "manageably uncomfortable" pace. As mentioned throughout this book, as we add stressors to our body, our body adapts. This rings true with gritervals. You will notice when you first start gritervalling, you need a lot of rest between repeats. About 6 weeks into consistent gritervalling, you will notice that you are mentally and physically ready to run the next interval before your beginning of season rest time has transpired. You will also see your griterval times improve throughout the training season provided you are consistent.

Warm-Up Cool-Down Sandwich—With these types of speed workouts and races for that matter, it's important that you always do warm up and cool down mileage. They both should be run at conversation pace. Our taxed breathing mileage should be saved for the meat of the sandwich; the gritervals. This is where the quality of the workout will reside. The purpose of the warm up mileage is to get your body warmed up and your mind ready to "drop the hammer." Warm up mileage also helps with our "plumbing". The purpose of the cool down mileage is to bring your heart rate back down to normal and to get your blood flowing back from the legs to the heart. Easy cool down mileage also helps to minimize muscle cramping.

Meet First-Timer, Joshua M

One word to describe my first marathon:
Beautiful

I first became interested in running a marathon because of the major marathon that happened every year in Chicago, the city I lived in. I continued to be inspired by people I knew and met as I pursued my interest. Around this same time, I met my coach and friend Denise who was, to say the least, an avid runner who also did coaching on the side. I actually met her when she opened a bank account and my old company. You see, she planted the marathon seed way back then. She inspired and encouraged me to run my first marathon, though at that point the idea had only been a thought and consideration. Then, a buddy said he wanted to run it as well, and that confirmed it. I decided that training for the marathon was something I should do. However, the year I signed up for my first Marathon was also my first year of running. Frustratingly, after the third week of training, I had to stop because of extreme pain in both lower legs—the cause of which I then discovered was compartment syndrome. I still ran my first marathon painstakingly because I was unable to train for it. I had the surgery that following March on both legs and successfully trained that year for my second marathon.

I think that if you want to do a marathon you can—one hundred percent. No matter how long it takes. Since I was not able to train for my first marathon I already knew it would be a hard push. Yet, I took away a valuable experience—I know the difference in how the muscles will be if you do or do not train for a marathon properly. After proper training, I remember how empowered and amazing it felt being able to run and not stop. I learned how you can mentally push the body to accomplish things. After my first and second marathon, I knew that I wanted to continue to run more of them. My goal is to run the big six marathons— Chicago, Boston, New York, Tokyo, Berlin, and London—but in general I plan to continue to run about four or five marathons a year.

One thing that really surprised me when I ran my second marathon was how much better the race is when you properly train for it.

Mile 20: Your Cheat Sheet for Your Final

Chapter focus: Why the 20-miler is so important in preparing you for race day.

Remember when you were in school and you were studying (for me it was more like cramming) for your final? You studied, but you oh so wished that you were given some hints as to what would be on the big test? Well, unlike most of your teachers, I am going to give you a cheat sheet for your final exam! That cheat sheet is your 20-mile long run. It is the perfect preview of coming attractions for what to expect on race day. During this milestone run, you will get the chance to test out one last time, your nutrition, hydration, go-to mantras, gear, pacing and even recovery regimen. It is the perfect time to put into play everything that you have been doing before, during and after your long runs.

For most of my first-timers, I recommend that they complete at least one 20-mile run. However, if they have been running strong throughout the season and also have a strong running base that they started the season with, I increase their longest run distance from 20 to 22 miles.

These extra miles are an even greater confidence boost that they have in their hydration belt come marathon morning. For my more experienced marathoners, I have them run two to three 22-mile runs in their training.

I recommend running your 20-miler three weeks before your marathon. It is in the last three weeks leading up to your marathon that you taper--more on tapering and the tantrums that come with it in the next Mile. As I mentioned in Mile 4, sometimes life will happen and get in the way of our training. You may have to push your 20-miler to two weeks before your marathon. If that is the case, don't fret! I would rather have you have a 20-miler under your belt with one less week of recovery time, than have you skip your 20-miler all together. To counteract losing that extra down week, I would recommend you incorporate more of your go-to recovery practices in your shortened taper, than if you had the full three weeks to taper. When I have to cut my taper down to two weeks or less, I incorporate not one but two 90-minute deep tissue massages the week before the marathon. Then marathon week, I get two 60-minute massages. During those two weeks, I also foam roll so much that I might as well sleep with my foam roller.

Just like the days leading up to your marathon, during the days leading up to your 20-miler, you want to ramp up on your sleep and your hydration (water and electrolytes). Also, make sure to have your marathon eve meal and marathon morning meal with this long run. Once you get started on your 20-miler, use the same type and quantity of nutrition/hydration that you will be using on race day. You will want to practice one last time with your anti-chafing and anti-blister tools of choice too. If there is anything new that you want to try before race day, now is the time to do it. For instance, do you want to try a new chafing glide or gel that your running mates successfully use. Did you stumble on a nipple chafing hack on the internet that you want to try? One of my clients uses a popular medical tape on his nipples instead of the normal store-bought guards. He said the tape stays on longer than the guards and it is sweat resistant. You are prone to getting muscle cramps and heard about a new liquid product that stops cramps in their tracks? Do you try it on this run? The answer is yes! It's better to try things out on this run then during your marathon. You will see that even on race day, you will still be fine tuning what works and what doesn't work for you.

You may be wondering why this last long run is not 26.2 miles. I thought the same thing. I actually thought that I needed to run more than 26 miles in training to ensure that my body could handle race day. I caution running more than 22 miles, as it puts you at risk for an injury. One reason that you only need to build up to a 20-mile run is because you are completing it on very tired, overworked legs. If you had fresh, rested legs, you would be able to run further. Taking three weeks off to taper between this run and your marathon, re-charges your legs and mind to get your through that extra distance. For anyone who has had their computer lock up, your taper is like a control-alt-delete to unlock your over worked body and mind.

What is critical to remember with your 20-miler is that completing the distance is more important than your clock time and pace. This is the case, even if you have to walk some of the latter miles, if not all of the latter miles. For clock time, I would only focus at a macro level in running a faster second half than the first half. Just like we want to do on race day. The benefits of this negative split approach are explained in Mile 8. Using your 20-mile pace is a skewed predictor of how fast you will run in your marathon because you are running 20 on tired legs versus 26.2 on rested legs.

Completing your 20-miler is not just a mammoth physical accomplishment, it is also a huge psychological feather in your cap. After I finish my 20-mile runs, I feel extra invincible and ready to take on anything. Well, after I have my well-earned breakfast(s) and nap(s). Not many people can say that they had 20 miles for breakfast, baby! From my experience, the marathon is 80 percent mental and 20 percent physical. That is why this run is also practice for consciously being in our head for 20 miles. Remember when 14 miles seemed mammoth? After running your first 20, 20 won't seem so mammoth either.

I definitely do not recommend my first 20-mile experience to any marathoner; first-timer or many-timer. As I mentioned earlier, I didn't follow a training plan for my first marathon. I didn't even know that the pinnacle of marathon training builds up to a 20-miler. The week leading up to my first marathon, my longest run was a local half-marathon. The universe and my then-husband circumstantially, led me to my first 20-miler. I got into an argument with my then-husband on Friday of marathon weekend. I don't remember what we fought about, I just remember him saying to me that I will never finish the marathon. Out of that "fire in my belly feeling." I took to the streets of my neighborhood and diffused my belly, so to speak. I logged my first 20-miler less than 48 hours before my marathon! In retrospect, this helped explain why it hurt to walk up and down curbs and stairs the week following my marathon. It also showed that I had a future in ultra-running.

As mentioned in Mile 13, if the timing of this run coincides with a hot and/or humid day either move your run to a cooler day that week or run a short loop over and over instead of a long out and back route. You want this loop to include your home, car, restaurant or a store that can provide you with easy access to nutrition, hydration, ice and maybe even close proximity to a restroom. An option for getting through your 20-miler, is to find a local half-marathon and run 7 miles before the race. That way you will pass the miles running alongside other runners and you will have race support for the last 13 miles of your 20-miler.

Meet First-Timer, Valerie J

One word to describe my first marathon: Fulfilling

I ran my first half-marathon only six months before running my first full. Before that, I was only a recreational runner who occasionally did 5Ks. A marathon was on my bucket list to do before I was 30 but I thought you needed to do a few half-marathons before considering a full--turns out I was wrong! It wasn't until I met Coach Denise that I decided to sign up for my first marathon. At the time, Denise was coaching me for my first half-marathon. A couple months into training we were out after one of our speed workouts and Denise told me that if I signed up for a full marathon that spring that she would run the race with me.

If someone didn't think they could do it, I would suggest that they invest in a running coach or join a training group. You'll meet people of all ages/shapes/sizes training for the same thing. Coach, Denise had me run a 20-mile training run prior to the race, which she ran with me and tricked me into running 22 miles instead. Turns out she did the same thing to Christian B (Mile 12 First-Timer) when they ran his first *20-miler* together. I have to admit though, that 22-miler really gave me confidence going into the marathon.

Running my first marathon showed me that I could accomplish more than I thought I could. When I was training for my first marathon I fully planned on doing another. In fact, I think the only way I could finish my first was to think about my second. Now, I'll be training for my first international race and I can't help think about what country I should run in next.

If I could have a do over of my first marathon, I would make sure to put body glide all over my body and not just the obvious places-you'll chafe in places you never thought about!

Mile 21: It's Taper Time!

Chapter focus: How to survive the taper and why we need it

Congratulations! You made it through the hardest part of the *physical* training. Remember how overwhelming a 20-mile run seemed when you first saw your training plan? BOOM, not anymore! Welcome now, to the toughest part of the *mental* training: the taper. It's during your taper, that you give your body time to restore after 17 weeks of intense training. You don't completely stop running during the taper but you significantly bring the mileage down so that you can have the freshest, springiest legs on race day. You also use this time to get your mental muscle--your mind--ready for race day. Be warned though, tapering does not come easy. Part of the problem is that your body and mind have been conditioned to run, run, run since you hit "submit" on the race website. Now, you need to re-program your body and mind to just run, rest and restore. This will ensure that you are truly race-ready at the start line. My friends and family can tell when I am in taper mode. I start straightening up their homes when I stop by. My apartment is immaculate. My cat, Stuey and my dog, Farley have been bathed. I am just a little short tempered, especially when waiting in line for my morning coffee.

To help minimize getting a case of the Taper Tantrums, follow some of my remedies below:

1. **My Peri-Endo-Maximus Hurts!** - If you haven't heard of that body part, that is because I made it up—an example of what our body and mind do to us when we are tapering. All of a sudden, we start having a weird ache in our hamstrings, knees, elbow, or insert any body part here, that we never felt during our training. Not even during our 20+ miler. We then start diagnosing ourselves on the internet and BAM, we automatically give ourselves a race day DNF when we haven't even toed the start line. This problem originates from the fact that we now have more time to spend in our heads than time spent out logging miles on our feet.

2. **The Hay is in the Barn** - It's important to know that extra mileage during this time is not going to improve your performance. Ironically, it may take away from your performance. The "Hay is in the Barn," so to speak. All of the hard work has been put in. You might even question if you put in enough mileage. You may tell yourself, "if only I had 'x' more weeks to train I would race a better marathon." Your race is right around the corner and - just like with a final exam - you feel like you need more time to study. However, cramming for this final exam will only hurt you. You need to save your legs for race day and trust your training.

3. **Stick With the Familiar** - It's also important not to do anything new during your taper that you haven't routinely done throughout your training. So, save Mile 26.3 for making friends with skydiving, high intensity interval training, rock climbing, yoga, etc. You have come too far to now get an injury, whether it's running or non-running related. You

might have the energy and the interest, but just hold off until post marathon.

4. **Restore** - After beating up your legs all season, they pretty much feel like concrete, right? To help get your legs loose and fresh for the start line, I recommend getting a massage shortly after your 20-miler and during the week leading up to the race. Keep up with your daily foam rolling. Now is also a great time to schedule your post marathon massage or whatever your go-to recovery treatment(s) have been.

5. **Remember me?!!** Now that you are not running as much, take advantage of your extra free time to reconnect with your friends and family. You have been gone for 17 weeks and they missed you. You can even get them logistically ready to hopefully come out and cheer you on race day. Now is also a great time to give back to you. So, catch up on that movie or book that has been calling your name. Or, if you are like me, hit the spa for that long-overdue pedicure.

Meet First-Timer, Kim H.

One word to describe my first marathon:
Exhilarating

I didn't start running with any regularity until I was 40. It was during one of my jogging phases that a friend at work started telling me about the races that she would run and invited me to run in a local 8K. My goal was to run the entire distance and I did. It was such a thrill to see my husband and daughters on the course cheering me on.

I continued to run regularly and through a half-marathon training group I had joined, I met some of the most positive, encouraging and motivating people I've ever known. They (including Coach Denise) would gently drop the hint that maybe I should consider running a marathon next. Denise made it clear that when I was ready, she would be there to guide me. Around this same time, I was coming up on 50 and though I never was one to care about age, there is something about milestone birthdays that gets you thinking. So, a decade after my first race, I put my name in the hat when the Chicago marathon lottery registration rolled around and left it to fate to decide!

I was inspired by my dad who was a very strong, active person his whole life but over the course of my training, he lost his ability to walk unassisted due to a neurological illness. As the miles got longer and the training got more difficult, I would think of my dad which in turn reminded me to appreciate my ability to run. I was also encouraged by my incredibly supportive family. Training for a marathon takes a lot of time and they never made me feel as if I was neglecting them. They never complained about my time away. After a particularly difficult training run, my husband then rode his bike with me on my next long run. He would meet me at various points along the way to make sure that I was properly fueled and hydrated. They were just as supportive on race day. They made posters, cheered me on at various spots on the course and they even threw me a little party afterwards complete with dinner and decorations, where I could re-live the events of the day.

As soon as I crossed the finish line of my first marathon, I knew I wanted to do it again. As of this writing, I am now signed up for my 3rd Chicago Marathon.

One thing that surprised me on race day was how much it helped to have friendly faces with me in the starting corral. I found that having someone to talk through those first-time jitters with was very helpful.

Mile 22: Go with the Flow

Chapter focus: Why you should run the mile that you are in and not fast forward to the final mile.

Have you ever done something spur of the moment? For example, you decide to go to a party at the last minute or decide to take a weekend getaway on Friday afternoon? How fun was that? Compare this to a vacation, concert, or black-tie event that you have planned for months. You can't wait, right? Then you take your vacation and it was just ok. The WOW-o-meter didn't not measure up to what you initially imagined. I think we have more fun when we do things last minute because our expectations are so low and we are more readily present. The experience is so last minute that we don't have time to set any expectations. Expectations can also be the root of disappointment when they do not meet our reality. This is why I am a big fan and practitioner of just going with the flow.

Let's translate this to racing. When I first started road racing, I would get so worried about whether I would be able to perform and get the time that I wanted. This worry is healthy in that it shows that I care about my performance and want to do well. But it is also counterproductive, in that I end up burning valuable energy that could have been funneled toward the execution of my performance. Even back in high school track, my stomach would be in knots all day worrying about racing against other runners and if I would be fast enough for my coach. When I started working with Coach Greg, I would stress every Wednesday worrying about what he would have us run for our track workout that night. I worried and stressed about whether I would be fast enough and about how much the workout was going to hurt to get through.

It wasn't until I ran my first marathon without a time goal that I experienced the power of just running the mile I was in instead of the cumulative 26.2 miles. It was the winter of 2005 and for some reason, I didn't get all of the quality training runs in that I normally would. Since I knew I wasn't in PR shape for racing Boston, I chose to just run it for fun that year. I know, that sounds like an oxymoron, right? Running Boston for fun. The night before the marathon, I did not have my typical spaghetti and marinara race-eve meal. I instead had pizza and beer! It was time to call it a night and my friends wanted to go. Since I was having so much fun and I wasn't going to race the next morning, I said, "just one more beer!" Fortunately, I listened to my friends and did not have that one more beer as that could have turned in to too many more.

With no clock pressure on myself, I ended up running my fastest Boston yet. I ran a 3:35! Wow, what a different experience that gave me with racing. When I *race* a race now, I still get a little angst in my stomach but it is about 5 percent of what it used to be. I think that is just human nature. Now when I race, I go with the flow, so to speak. I get into a zone in which my breathing is controlled and taxed. I find a "manageably-uncomfortable" pace. I look at my watch in the early miles to make sure that I am not starting out too fast. Once I finish, then I look at my overall time. If it's a PR, awesome; if not, it's still awesome because I know I gave my best. What a relief it is now to not have an ape on my back, putting self-inflicted pressure on my performance.

Meet First-Timer, Kelly H.

One word to describe my first marathon:
Empowering

I didn't have much of a background in running when I started because I began as an adult. I developed my love for the sport following a divorce in 2007. Running was my escape and gave me time each day to quiet my thoughts and just focus on one thing. When running harder or trying to go further, it is difficult to think about anything other than that very moment. I wanted to keep challenging myself and to attempt something I never thought I could do. So, I decided to sign up for my first marathon.

I learned so much about myself, my body, and my mind when training for my first marathon. I learned that I can push myself more than I ever could have imagined. If I want it bad enough, completing that challenge is the most amazing thing. I learned that my brain will give out and want to quit well before my body does.

I think I'm proof that people can take up running anytime and that anyone who wants to, most certainly can run a marathon. Too many people to list inspired me to run, but I think it was Coach Denise who helped keep my spirits up and kept me healthy. Proper coaching and doing your homework will get you to the end: my favorite part! I am one of those crazy people that loves the end of the race. I think miles 23-26.2 are always the best. As I crossed the finish line of my first marathon, there was no doubt in my mind that I would be doing a second.

If I could go back in time, I'd tell myself how much I'm going to love it so I could have started running sooner in life.

Mile 23: The World is Your Treadmill

*Chapter focus: Pack your running shoes; let's go experience
this big, blue marble, one foot strike at a time!*

Antarctica, Reykjavik, Tokyo, Sydney, Paris and Durban are just a few of
the destinations that I have RaceCationed in. A RaceCation is exactly what
it sounds like. You run a race on your vacation. You sacrifice with your
training and then you reward with a vacation. Having a destination race
gives you a little extra motivation to keep up with your training. When it
comes to your itinerary, I recommend scheduling your marathon on the
front end of your trip. Also, as I mentioned in Mile 24, make sure to carry
on all of your race day gear and nutrition with you on the plane.

I am the first to admit that I have an addiction to RaceCationing! How
can I not? It combines my love of running with my love of traveling. I get
to experience a new city on my feet, I meet other runners who also love
traveling and I return home with some new race bling and an experience
of a life time! RaceCationing also helps me carry out one of my lifelong
goals of getting as many passport stamps as I can before I die.

I bring out the RaceCation card in full force when I meet someone who hates running or when I meet someone who doesn't think they can do a marathon but secretly has it on their bucket list. The incentive to RaceCation in Paris is what motivated my client, Sara, (Mile 13 First-Timer) to sign up for her first marathon. When Sara first reached out to me for coaching, her goal was to lose weight through running. She wanted to commit to running with a coach two mornings a week. When we met, she had never run a race. On our runs, I would tell her about some of my favorite RaceCations and some of my upcoming marathon trips. Like most of my beginners, she had no idea that there were races all over the world. On one of our runs, I told her about Marathon Tours. They are a travel company based out of Chelsea, Massachusetts that bundles race entries, hotel accommodations and excursions for marathons and half-marathons across all 7 Continents. I have been traveling with them since my first RaceCation: Boston Marathon 1999.

It was on my first running session with Sara, that I planted the marathon seed. Six weeks later, that seed bloomed! Sara and I were on a run and she asked me if I knew there was a marathon in Paris. I couldn't believe she said the word marathon, let alone asked about a specific marathon. I gleefully smiled and said, "I did" and "I will run it with you!" Fast forward to April 2016; Sara, the girl who had never run a race in her life, trained for and ran the Paris Marathon! After we crossed the finish line, however, she did say that was the hardest thing she had ever done and that she would never do that again. I could *so* relate: circa 1994 Chicago Marathon. Twenty-four hours after she ran her first marathon, I received a text from her asking me if I knew there was a marathon in Bordeaux, France. Yes, indeed, I told her. I knew all about the Medoc Marathon. Never say never.

Out of all of the marathons that I have run, the most beautiful destination marathons were Antarctica, Reykjavik, Iceland and Big Sur, California. The only part of the Antarctica marathon that resembled Antarctica was the section of the course in which we had to run up a Glacier. The rest of the two-loop course was run on a gravel road near the Chilean, Russian, Chinese and Uruguayan scientific research bases. The race itself was such a small component of the trip. It was the exploring that we did before and after the race that led to this trip being my favorite trip of all. In the five days that we spent in the Antarctica peninsula, we rode zodiac rafts to get to shore. It was there that we came toe to feet with penguins. We also took the rafts in and out of icebergs and to an old whaling village. Every day seemed to blow away the day before in adventure and beauty. While we were at sea, the crew lectured on the history of Antarctica and on the wildlife. Exploring this White Continent was like being on your own Discovery Channel.

The Reykjavik, Iceland trip was similar to Antarctica in that after the marathon, we then explored the country. We rented an SUV and then drove around the whole country. We hiked a glacier. We rode Icelandic horses. We bathed in the Blue Lagoon. We climbed inside a volcano to see stalagmites first-hand. We rode zodiac rafts in and out of icebergs. We saw at least half a dozen waterfalls. Truly one of the most beautiful places that I have been.

My first Big Sur Marathon was in 2000. It was just weeks after running the Boston marathon. This was before you received a commemorative jacket of this double marathon feat. With Big Sur, it is not just the area around Big Sur that is beautiful but also the race itself. The race starts in the redwoods of Big Sur, California and traverses alongside the Pacific Ocean up to the city of Carmel. At the half way point, there is a gentleman in a tuxedo playing a grand piano. You can hear the music well before you come up upon the pianist. This is a very challenging course as you are running up and down mountains. However, the views are so beautiful that you forget how much your legs hurt. They say that you should not focus on getting a personal record on this course but instead focus on having a good time. I definitely had a good time at both of my Big Sur marathons.

There are marathons all over the world just waiting for you to run. You can run a marathon on the North Pole, in Madagascar and even on the Great Wall to name a few. As I type this, I am thinking of a few of my bucket list marathons of Patagonia, Mt Everest Base Camp and Kilimanjaro. When you are looking for extra motivation to train and/or commit to a marathon, find yourself a destination marathon. The marathon becomes the excuse to visit this new city. Then, once you arrive, you start exploring à pied. There are even a handful of marathon distinctions you can achieve through RaceCationing:

50 States Marathon Club—Completing a marathon in all 50 states

Seven Continents Club—Completing a marathon on each continent

Seven Marathons in Seven Days on Seven Continents—Completing a marathon on each continent in only seven days

Abbott World Marathon Majors Six Star Finisher—Completing all Six of the Abbott World Marathon Major Marathons. This includes the Tokyo, Boston, London, Berlin, Chicago and New York Marathons.

Marathon Grand Slam—Completing a marathon on all seven continents and the North Pole

100 Marathon Club North America - You complete 100 marathons/ultra-marathons

Meet First-Timer, Susie R.

One word to describe my first marathon:
Surreal/Addicting

I dabbled in running before my first marathon, usually only running 3 miles. Those 3 miles I considered a huge success (because it is!). Growing up a competitive swimmer, I never considered running my talent. The natural skill, strength, and success I had in the water never translated to the land. Even now, I barely consider myself a runner. But still, when my friend encouraged me to join her running group, I was hooked. There was no pressure, there was no pace expectation, and they had one goal - to feel better at the finish than they did at the start. I just kept showing up and after a while I decided that I better find myself a spot in the marathon!

That perspective really made it possible for me to run. I'd tell anyone who was starting to train to start slow and just focus on finishing. Take each week at a time and relish in how much more your body can do. Eventually, you build the mileage up and before you know it, you will be describing a 4-mile run as "going out for a quick jog."

I viewed the marathon as an experience where I took in all the different neighborhoods, laughed at the funny signs, thanked the volunteers, and smiled at the spectators who yelled my name and encouraged me to keep going. I kept that smile on my face from start to finish. If I had been hard on myself or criticized myself, I don't know if I would have finished. But I wasn't running for time. I was just running to finish and to raise funds for Team PAWS Chicago. Running the marathon meant I got to fundraise to save the lives of the homeless pets in Chicago. They inspired me to keep going.

One thing that surprised me on race day was how much time it takes to get across the start line when you are in one of the last corrals - I would have brought a snack to eat while waiting!

Mile 24: Finals Week

*Chapter focus: A rundown of last minute preparations
for race day.*

At the risk of sounding like a broken record, I am risking it! DJ Denise is
playing that song again. The "hay is in the barn." Any additional mileage
you run on top of what is in your training plan, could negatively affect
race day performance. You have come too far to risk an injury now,
let alone compromise rested legs. This week, it is all about getting your
body, mind and cheer squad, ready for 26.2, baby! Since you are still in
taper mode, you are probably suffering from too much free-time on your
plate. Instead of letting your race nerves get the best of you, shift that
energy toward getting lots of rest and hydration, while also avoiding any
new activities or nutrition. You are precious cargo. Meaning, that this
week, you just say "no" to rock climbing, go-karting, skydiving even yoga
if it hasn't been a part of your day to day throughout this training season.

One very important tip that I want to stand out above the rest is for
those of you who are flying to your marathon: make sure that you have

your race day shoes, gear and nutrition with you when you board the plane. Do not pack these into a checked bag. If the airline loses your bag, you will then have to try and recreate your race day outfit and nutrition upon arrival.

T-7 days thru T-1 day until your marathon:

Mile 0—I treat the start corral as if it were a departure gate. I plan extra time to get to the airport so that once I am there I have at least an hour to sit at the gate and chillax. I treat race starts the same way. That being said, I recommend that you spend the early days of this week getting familiar with when your race corral opens and closes, how you are getting to the start line and at what time. If you are driving to the start, predetermine parking options and be aware of street closures. If you need to take a race designated bus, get familiar with the logistics? If you are nervous in any way about the course because you have never seen or run on it before, I would recommend driving the course before race day to help give you a preview of coming attractions. This is especially the case if the terrain will be more extreme than the terrain that you trained on. For instance, when I ran the Comrades Marathon in summer of 2018, I made sure to tour the route ahead of time. That course was extremely hilly compared to my Chicago lakefront. Seeing the course ahead of time may help release some of pre-race angst and also help with visualizing race day.

Packing—Just like you would not want to pack for your flight the day of your trip, you also do not want to pack for the marathon on marathon eve, let alone marathon morning. You can use Aid Station 3 to help guide you. Look over the list and check it twice. That way, if you forgot something, you have days and not hours to hunt down the missing item(s). Then you can add them to your carefully crafted race day carry on. As mentioned at the start of this mile, if you are flying to a race city, make sure to place your race day gear and nutrition in your carry on. You do not want to take any chances with your checked bag(s) getting lost.

If race morning is projected to be cold but then warm up, pack throw away clothes that will keep you warm while you are waiting in the start corral. Right before your start, you can then toss these clothes. I usually use a zip up sweatshirt or a mylar blanket from one of my prior finish lines to help stay warm. If I can't find a zip up, I will transform a long sleeve shirt into a "V" neck with scissors so that it is easy to take off while running. If it's going to be a cold morning, I also bring throw away gloves and hand warmers.

If you do not already have your name on your shirt and are pressed for time, I recommend that you just use bright colored duct tape and a permanent marker. Take two strips of the duct tape and place it on the front of your shirt. Write your name in large letters on the duct tape. Having your name on the front of your shirt is especially helpful in the latter miles of your race. You get so much energy hearing your name, even though you may not even now the people calling it out. This will put an extra spring in your step. It's hard to describe this feeling in words. You just have to experience it.

DJ Denise is back in the house once again, reminding you, that you should minimize trying anything new on race day, especially shoes, nutrition or socks. Even if you just replaced your shoes at the expo with the exact same model and size that you trained in. These shoes are not broken in yet and you do not want to break them in marathon morning.

Nighty, Night—Along with hydration and recovery, it's also important to load up on those Zzzzzzs race week. As race day approaches and our anxiety level increases, our quality and quantity of sleep will decrease. Proper sleep will allow for a sound body and mind to "Slay the Day!"

Yum in My Tum—For race week nutrition, stick with what has worked on your long runs. From my own painful experience, just say no to Penne Arribiata on marathon eve! Yes, this veteran marathoner did not listen to her own advice at the 2014 Schaumburg Marathon. Let's just say, I had to make at least 10 pit stops in addition to hydration stops. I was not able to get into a running groove until mile 22! My go-to pre-race meal has always been plain pasta with marinara sauce. I mistakenly thought having pasta with a little kick would be ok. My stomach thought different. Now, I know to stick exactly to my already tried and true routine. Since I have trained with carbo-loading, I start carbo-loading three nights before the marathon. I add protein (chicken breast) to my pasta only on the 2nd and 3rd nights leading up to the marathon. Marathon eve, I just have plain pasta since I have found that protein the night before leads to GI issues during the race. As I mentioned in Mile 6, everybody's body is different. So, having protein on marathon eve may work for you. If steak dinner the night before your long run has worked then stick with steak. Marathon eve, I try not to eat any later than 6:00 PM. This ensures that my "plumbing" will be taken care of before I cross that start line. If you are running a marathon such as Boston or New York City Marathon, they start later than most marathons. I move my pre-race dinner to 8:30 PM local time for these races.

Cheers!—Similar to the carbo-loading concept for race week, I recommend hydration loading. During the marathon, we lose a lot of water and electrolytes through our sweat. This is especially the case if the temperature is hot. It's important to not just increase your water intake but to also increase your electrolytes intake. Whatever electrolyte hydration you used during your workouts, stick with that race week. As a reminder, if you are going to use course hydration/electrolytes make sure that you have tried it during your long runs

What you See, You Will Achieve—In addition to getting your body ready for 26.2, this week you should also focus on getting your mind ready. Use this time to go back through your training log and see how far you have come. Remember when 13 miles seemed scary? Not anymore! Visualize how race morning and race day will be. Especially plan ahead for when the race actually starts; the wall. You can negatively curse at your wall and try to wish it away. This is coming from my own personal experience. Or you can positively and consciously embrace it. Reciting my mantras as well as my gratitude alphabet help me to embrace and power through my wall. I remind myself that it is the wall that makes the marathon medal worth its weight in gold and the lactic acid that built up on my muscles worth the Frankenstein crawl the days after the marathon. For if it was easy and comfortable, everyone would be a marathoner, right?

T-4 days until your marathon:

What You Knead—After 20 weeks of go, go, going mentally and physically, getting a massage this week will help give your body and mind a beneficial reset. There are three caveats to getting a massage this week. One, if you have not had a massage all season, this would not be a good time to start. Secondly, if you do get a massage this week, make sure to let the massage therapist know that you are "x" days out from running your first marathon. That way they will not go too deep on your muscles. Lastly, I recommend that you get your massage anytime between the Monday and Thursday of race week. Provided the marathon is on Sunday. You do not want to have the massage too close to race day. When you have your massage this week, it is also a good time to schedule your post marathon massage for either the day after your marathon or two days after if you have not scheduled one already. This week is also a great time to keep up with foam rolling. The looser and more relaxed we can get our body before we toe the start line, the better!

Cue the Tunes—If you run with music, now is a perfect time to make a new playlist. What a nice treat that would be to get some fresh tunes instead of same ole, same ole. Some of my friends even run to movie and musical soundtracks. To make sure you have your music from start to finish, make sure to put your phone on airplane mode and do not disturb to save battery power. I also download my songs to my phone so that I don't have to stream them and drain even more battery power. Another option is to run with an extra battery pack. This logistic is definitely something you do not want to be dealing with on marathon eve, so take advantage of your down time to create your race day tunes!

Fan Club Prep—It's best to use the days leading up to the marathon and not the day before the marathon to field phone calls, texts and emails from your cheer squad of where they should be on the course, where can they park, where can they find coffee and brunch, etc. After looking at the course map, I try to position my cheer squad at mile markers that have us loop back on to the same intersections. For instance, at mile 3 you may be running on the west side of Main & Lake Street and then on mile 8 you then head back east on the Main & Lake. That way your fans get a two-for-one spot by going to mile 3 and then subsequently crossing the street to mile 8. I recommend that you tell your crew ahead of time to one, sign up for runner tracking if the race offers it and two, for the mile markers that your cheer squad will be at, predetermine if they should stand on the "runners right" side of the course where that mile marker is or on the "runners left" side. This way, as you approach the predefined mile marker, you will easily be able to see them. It will be easier for you to spot your fan than it will be for them to spot you amongst a sea of runners. Another way to help find your squad amongst all of the spectators is to have them hold a brightly colored, obnoxious balloon or umbrella. If you can only have your cheer squad at one point on the course, I encourage you to send them to mile 21 or later. You want them in these latter miles. Those are the miles where you need the most encouragement. You should also designate a post-marathon meet-up spot ahead of time. Most marathons will have a family reunite area right after you exit the finish line zone. There are usually large signs for each letter of the alphabet in the reunite area.

T-2 days until your marathon:

Hello, My Name Is—I have another analogy for races that I have not shared yet. To me, a race is just like a party. You RSVP. You go with your friends and make more friends. You have cocktails (water and electrolytes). Some parties have live music. You sometimes get gifts at a party; medal and race shirt. You can elevate your heart rate at parties from dancing while at races your heart rate elevates from running. Lastly, you get a name tag at some parties. For your 26.2 party, your race bib becomes your name tag.

In getting your race day name tag, I recommend that you go to the race expo two days if not three days before the race. The closer it gets to race day, the more crowded that the expo will be. Not to mention, the longer the expo goes on, the more likely they will sell out of the marathon gear in the early days. To make sure that you get the size gear that you want,

I would get to the expo as early as you can. Most races require that you show an ID in order to pick up your race packet. Make sure that you pack your ID when heading there. One additional warning is that you should avoid posting pictures on social media of your race bib for popular races. Runners that did not get into the race could make a Do It Yourself bib from your bib photo. This is especially common with Boston.

Mind Your Gap—There was a method to my madness in wanting you to log your workouts. We touched on this in Mile 7. When looking for inspiration, you just need to look in the mirror and at your training log. Look at how far you have come. Look at how many miles you ran this season. Take note of your personal milestones. Maybe it was your highest mileage week, your fastest mile, your fastest quarter mile, your 18-miler that you ran and felt like you could have done more. Draw on these milestones that you would have missed out on if you didn't put in the training. They always tell us not to look back, as there is nothing that we can do about the past. In marathon training though, I encourage you to look in the rear-view mirror! Unless we take the time to go back and look at our logs, we lose sight of how far we have come and how much we have achieved before we even toe the start line.

T-1 day until your marathon:

Nighty, Night, Take 2!—It's important to sleep in as much as you can the morning before the marathon to make up for not being able to sleep in race morning. No one gets sleep the night before the race that's why you should try and sleep-in the day and days before your marathon. If you have trouble sleeping, some of my go-tos that help me get some shut-eye are listening to a mediation app, podcast or a book that I have been itching to read but haven't had the time to crack open.

Shake that Angst!—To help shake some of the pre-race nerves, I recommend that you run an easy 2.62 -miles (get it?) the day before your marathon. You can even use this shakeout run to scope out the lay of the land for your start and finish line.

Meet First-Timer, Andrea T.

One word to describe my first marathon:
Inspiring

My first race was a 5k Pumpkin Chase. I was 8 years old at the time and ran it with my dad. From the moment I finished that race, I was hooked. I'll never forget how strong and how free I felt. As a result, I had a pretty successful high school cross-country and track career. I continued to run races and jog for overall health in college and early adulthood. Several years back, I developed a bucket list chock full of experiences that would challenge me in all sorts of ways. Running a marathon was one of the first items on my list, but my father's diagnosis with Stage III renal cell carcinoma on April 1, 2009, made me realize it was time. After the initial shock wore off, I signed up for the Chicago Marathon and chose to run for the Kidney Cancer Association in honor of my amazing dad.

As I write this, I'm three weeks out from my third Marathon—this time running alongside a first-timer at her pace and rallying to get her through. I cannot wait to run it with her and experience that magic of a first marathon through her eyes.

Everyone seems to focus so much on the physical part of running when they get started, but so much of it is mental. Yes, 26.2 miles is a long way. Yes, it's going to be a struggle. Yes, you likely will want to stop at some point. But it's remarkable what you can do when you set your mind to it. The resulting confidence and strength that comes from pushing yourself in this manner only makes you stronger and better—even in your everyday life. I really came to realize just how therapeutic and spiritual running is. It's more than just getting in shape for me. It's my place to lose myself in my thoughts, connect with nature, and even connect with my own spirituality.

One thing that I learned at my first marathon and after months and months of training is that the race is the easy part—I had fun!

Mile 25: Your Final Exam - Race Day!

Chapter focus: How to ace your final and have fun on your victory lap to 26.2!

Even though your SCITED meter may be hovering strongly in the scared zone, that is completely normal. After all, you have never done this before. I am here to help you turn that anxiousness to excitement. It's not every day you run your first marathon! I won't lie, I have been waiting for this day since you hit submit on the race registration website! Know that you are not alone. There will be lots of fellow first-timers at the start line with you. Not to mention there will be a lot of "many-timers" there too that finished their first and continue to keep coming back for more. Let's do your 26.2!

First off, since you can never recreate your first marathon, I recommend that you take in as much as you can. Throw clock time out the window for the most part and focus on a good time. Your marathon should start out fun, get funner and end being the funnest thing you have done in a long time! If you are like the rest of us, you will have plenty of other marathons to focus on clock time. The beauty of the marathon, whether it is your first or 100th, is that you will experience so many emotions race day; fear, excitement, rockstar-ness, pain, doubt, gratitude, empowerment, etc. For me, I never know which emotions will rise to the top, let alone know when they will rise. It's pretty epic to be able to experience so many different emotions in one day. Enjoy your emotional rollercoaster ride!

BEFORE THE RACE:

- To help your Cheer Squad find you on the course, text them a picture of you in your race gear.

- Remember nothing new today. Eat the same brand of oatmeal that you've been eating before your long runs—instead of suddenly switching to a hard-boiled egg, for instance. And absolutely do not wear the new shoes you bought at the expo. Can you say ouch? Today is not the day to break them in.

- If you have a particular nutrition that is not on the course, give extra to your cheer squad in case you lose any nutrition that you are running with.

- Check the weather one last time. Remember that the weather is one of the two things we can't control on race day. The other being our stomach. That being said, if you have unfavorable conditions just remember that everyone else will be tolerating the same weather and are probably having the same cursing thoughts. Think about the volunteers that are also putting up with the same non-runner friendly weather.

  - If it's too hot or humid remember to throw pace out the window and focus more on safely getting to the finish line. When it's extremely hot out, I carry a zip lock bag and then look for ice cubes on the course. Holding the bag with the ice cubes in it, helps to keep my body temperature down. I will collect ice at aid stations and from spectators. If I see a cooler on the course, I basically trick or treat to fill my bag with ice. I also have my cheer squad carry a cooler with bags of ice ready to hand off to me.

- As a reminder, if it's chilly on marathon morning, bring throw-away clothes to keep warm in for the start corral and race village. If you don't want to throw clothes away, then wear an extra-large garbage bag or a mylar blanket from a prior race.

- Get to the race village early because you don't want to have to sprint to your start corral. Remember this is your flight to Marathon Land!

  - Run an easy 5 minutes out and 5 minutes back warm-up to help you shake off some anxiety and to help take care of your "plumbing."

  - If you need to use a porta-potty, I recommend that you get in line after dropping off your gear bag. Once you use the porta-potty, get back in line again. The lines will get longer as the race start gets closer.

Mile 0 ALL THE WAY TO Mile 26.2:

- As exciting as your first marathon is, try to get keep your breathing controlled. Use that as a metronome to get into a relaxed rhythm.

- If you don't already do a run/walk interval, add a walk interval from the start of the race. Even if that walk interval is 60 seconds at each aid station or 2 minutes at each mile marker. I have a saying (and race day hack) that it's better to walk when you *want* to then when you *have* to. If you wait until you have to, it will be too hard to restart running from a walk break. This is from my own experience. I take a 30-60 second walk break at each mile. Then when I get to mile 20 or so, if my legs feel strong, I drop the walk interval. As, I mentioned in Mile 8, when you do walk, walk with a purpose. Walk as if you have to go to the bathroom and you can't find one!

- Thank the volunteers and the emergency staff out on the course. Even high five the spectators. They are supporting us in achieving our goal. More than likely they have been out on the course longer then we have. Not to mention you never know who you will inspire that day.

- If you are running with a pace group, be aware that while they do their best, they may or may not hit the pace goal. If you're looking at your watch and their times are off, don't be afraid to drop away from the group and be your own pacer. Remember this is your race.

- Consistently throughout the race, I recommend that if you are going to rely on the aid stations on the course, go to the end of the aid stations where they are less crowded. I also recommend that you alternate between water and the electrolyte fluids. Too much of one or the other could cause hyponatremia or GI issues, respectively.

- Review my pacing suggestions to help you stay reserved and run a negative split marathon.

- To minimize the overwhelming-ness of 26.2 freackin' miles, break the marathon into pieces by using some of these tips:

  - Break the race down in to 4 separate 10Ks (with some "change") and then focus on one 10K at a time.

  - Dedicate a mile to someone in your circle and then focus on one mile at a time.

  - If you are running your marathon for a charity, dedicate a mile to one of your donors and then focus on one mile at a time.

  - Run the first half of the marathon with your head (stay reserved) and the second half with your heart (grit, baby!).

- If at any time during the marathon you feel faint, are in extreme pain or are just not feeling it, stop and seek help. There will be a lot more marathons for you to run but there is only one you. Listen to your body. In the summer of 2012, I was competing in my third Ironman triathlon. When I compete in a triathlon, I aim to be the last athlete in the water. This minimizes my swim anxiety. In that triathlon, I was the last athlete in the water for my race category. However, there were two more categories of athletes behind me that translated to 300 plus swimmers trailing me in the water. I was able to swim for about 45 minutes of the 2.4-mile swim but after that I could not get my heart rate down. I was anxious from the water being churned up by the swimmers that were once behind me catching up and passing me. My anxiety level was getting worse as some of the swimmers started swimming on top of me. At this point, I knew I still had another hour to swim. No matter what Zen conversation I tried telling myself, I could not relax. I made an executive decision to get pulled out of the water and I took a DNF for the race. At first, I felt like a loser because what kind of coach quits a race? I didn't stay in this self-deprecating state very long as I reminded myself that as athletes we need to listen to our bodies and take responsibility for our own safety. I ended up turning in my race chip. Since I trained for the event, I still continued on and road the bike course and did the run. I also wear the race shirt with pride even though I wasn't an official finisher. It's a reminder that I tried, raced smart and still went on with my day to day life with a DNF.

- Since I rarely run the exact route that the marathon course was measured on, my GPS watch tends to signal a mile split before I even hit the course's mile marker. I finish the marathon with sometimes 27 miles on my GPS watch. To help see my actual mile splits, I wear a sports watch and a

GPS watch. I start them both as soon as I cross that start line. I wear the former to know my exact mile pace.

MILES 0 TO Mile 20: The Warm-Up Miles

- This is the EXCITING part of SCITED. You can feel the energy coming off the crowd as well as the fellow marathoners alongside you. You feel like the Grand Marshal in your own parade. I am cautioning you though, that this is also the time that you want to stay reserved in your pacing. Make sure that you are not running your 5K and 10K pace during these miles. Save that for the last 5K and 10K. It might be hard to hold back because your taper gave you fresh, ready-to-go legs. Not to mention, you have the "Wahoo, this is awesome!" vibe. You know that you are now hours away from becoming a marathoner. To help "cool your jets," pretend like I am alongside you on my megaphone repeating, the "marathon doesn't start until mile 20. The marathon doesn't start until mile 20!" Don't get caught up in runners passing you. Let them go ahead. More than likely you will pass most of them later since they do not hear my megaphone 411. Knowing that the race will be mentally tougher from mile 20 on, save some spring in your step for these miles. You need to decide if you want to be the passer in these miles or the passee.

- If you know that the early aid stations are going to be crowded, I recommend that you carry a throw away hydration bottle so that you can skip these stations and hydrate on your own.

MILES 20 TO Mile 26.2: When the Marathon Really Starts!

This is the part of the race that makes the medal worth its weight in grit. You have just entered the infamous Wall. Most runners dread it, but I say you should welcome it. That's when you will need to dig deep and find that inner mojo you didn't know you had. Getting past the wall is what makes this day so life-electrifying and that medal worth it all. It's also why everyone isn't a marathoner. It is this inner fight and grit that separates us from those who never try.

These miles are also the point in the marathon when your mind is telling your legs to move and your legs have selective hearing and are choosing not to listen. They are moving but slowly. It's also the point where the mile markers are not coming up as fast as they once were. Throughout your training though, you have prepared for these miles. Anytime you didn't want to run and you did, you strengthened your mental endurance. Any time the weather forced you to run on the dreadmill, you strengthen your mental endurance. It's also in these miles that you might have a bad radio channel or playlist streaming in your head telling you that you can't do it or that you should quit. We both know that on the other side of this discomfort is the magic. So, when this bad playlist comes on, I recommend the following:

- Go through your mantras.

- Remind yourself how far you have come physically and mentally since you started training.

- Cheer on the runners next to you and maybe help each other get to the finish together.

- Remember your Why.

- Visualize all of the hard workouts that you fought through and draw inner strength from them.

- Go through your Gratitude Alphabet.

- Focus on one step at a time or getting to one light post, the person in the bright colored shirt, the upcoming intersection, etc. at a time. Find a landmark on the course not far in front of you and focus on getting there, then finding another one and another one, etc.

- Count your steps from 1 to 100. You will get lost into the count and your legs will follow your mind.

- Remind yourself that the pain is temporary and the accomplishment is permanent.

- Hopefully you will run into your Cheer Squad during these miles. Just seeing them you will light up on the inside and get indescribable energy from them. Again, this is a feeling that I can't truly explain until you go through it.

Mile 26.2: That Magical Finish Line, Baby!

- Don't be surprised if you cry at the finish line. I've done it and I know why—it's because you just tapped into something within you that you didn't even know existed. Not to mention, you just ran a FREACKIN marathon! Take that gym teacher!

- My only word of warning with the finish line is to make sure that you are not stopping your watch as you cross the finish line. This makes for not the best race photo. There more than likely will be race photographers waiting to capture your marathon moment at the finish line, so instead of getting a picture of you looking at your watch, raise those hands in the air in triumph. You just did what you once thought was impossible! Let your race chip capture your precise clock time and just stop your watch post-race photographers.

- Now it's time to get your hard-earned medal and official race photos taken. To save money for the next race entry or airfare for your next destination race, you can ask a fellow runner or volunteer to take some Do It Yourself finish pictures.

POST RACE: Mile 26.2 and Change!

- How 'bout that finish line, baby?! That wasn't as bad as you thought, right? You are now part of the 1 percent of the population that has run a marathon. You are in da Club!

- Continue walking as much as you can. I know that this is the last thing that you will want to do but think of it as a short-term sacrifice for a week-long reward. Walk as much as you can after you finish and prolong sitting down as long as you can. Once you sit, your muscles will tighten up and walking will be even more challenging!

- Hydrate and refuel to help with your recovery nutrition or hydration go to of choice. Just like in your long runs, you want to refuel with your go to recovery drink or meal of choice within 20 to 30 minutes.

- To help mitigate muscle soreness, I recommend a massage and or ice bath. Some marathons even offer complimentary massages post finish line. If that is the case, definitely take advantage of this perk. Just give them a heads-up not to go deep on your muscles because you just beat them up enough getting to the finish line.

- If you were given a post-race blanket or poncho, don't toss it when you are done with it. Instead, save it for your next cold start corral.

- Connect and thank your cheer squad! Most of them have been alongside this journey since you hit submit on the registration website.

- Reward!

Meet First-Timer, Peter S.

One word to describe my first marathon: Moving

Inspired by my older brother's enjoyment on the high school cross-country team, my running career began in eighth grade when I joined him on the team. I ran throughout high school and for three years of college. I was never an elite runner but I enjoyed the challenge of competing against others and myself. In recent years, as work and other life priorities arose, and the structure of running on a team disappeared, I found myself making less and less time to run.

Persistence made me sign up for my first marathon. Not *my* persistence, but the persistence of a *certain second cousin*—Coach Denise—who implored me to sign up. Additionally, the 2016 Chicago marathon fell on the one-year anniversary of the passing away of my father, so I committed to run it in his memory. The rest of my family have been the biggest motivation as I felt running this race in memory of my dad was just as much for them, as it was for me. My dad, although gone from this world, will always be an inspiration for me to challenge myself.

I think anyone can complete a marathon with two tools: faith in yourself and a support network made up of family, friends, running buddies, or coach. That being said, I wouldn't recommend running a marathon without a good training program—if I had been more consistent in training, I would have been happier with my finish time. The only goal I had for my first marathon was to finish the race and enjoy it. It may sound weird to say that you can 'enjoy' running 26.2 miles but when you have tens of thousands of fellow runners and hundreds of thousands of spectators, just being a part of that experience is a blast! Even before running the marathon, I knew there'd be more in my future as I feel compelled to complete all of the six major marathons at some point.

One thing that surprised me on race day were all of the people that I didn't even know that would be cheering us on, high fiving us, holding up awesome signs and of course that runners high I experienced at the end is right up there too. I had no idea how fun the actual race was going to be!

Mile 26.2 What Next?

Chapter focus: What's next after passing Marathoning 101.

Stay SCITED

I want you to think about how you felt when you first signed up for the marathon and then compare that to how you feel now as a M.A.R.A.T.H.O.N.E.R. You went from SCITED to downright invincible right? That is the transformative gift that facing our fears rewards us with. A soul-awakening gift that can't be bought but must be earned. All it took was the courage to try, a syllabus and a lot of homework. I want you to draw from this experience the next time you don't think you can do something and just try. We never know what else we have in us until we try. As I mentioned in Mile 2, my first marathon led me to triathlons, skydiving, starting my own consulting business, improv classes and the most uber first, "de-corporating" and becoming a full-time running coach. Stay SCITED, my friend!

Get Moving

To help your body recover from the stress we just put it under and increase the blood flow to your muscles, I recommend that you jog or speed walk the two days following your marathon. You only need to jog/walk for 15 minutes each day. The longer we sit still, the tighter our muscles will get. If you have access to a pool, swimming is an even better option. In addition to getting your body moving, I also recommend that you get a deep tissue massage after your marathon. Just make sure to let the massage therapist know that you just ran a marathon. Don't forget to plant the "marathon seed" and let them know that they too can do a marathon. Focus too on rehydrating in the days after your marathon. For additional information on recovery, revisit Mile 10.

Post Marathon Blues (PMB)

How can you not be sad that the marathon is over? Your time and energy has been focused on this personal goal of yours for twenty plus weeks. Now your day to day, night to night focus has lost its focus. Not to mention, once you get a taste of that euphoric feeling mile 26.2 gives you, you want to feel it again! PMB is a real thing and I have a cure for it! Find another race! Whether it be another marathon or even a 5K. For the former, I recommend that you wait at least 6 weeks before running another one and make sure that you are properly recovered from your first marathon. I promise you that you will be so much lighter the second time around angst-wise. This is because there are less unknowns and you now know that YOU CAN DO IT! Running a 5K or even a half-marathon now will be a piece of cake compared to 26.2. You can even take a break from racing and instead use some of your free time to volunteer at an upcoming race or even help someone in your circle get started with running or walking. Another way to pay it forward is by volunteering as a running guide with organizations like Achilles International or Dare2tri.

Got Bling?

How sweet is that new piece of hardware around your neck? One of my favorite parts about marathon weekend is seeing fellow finishers wearing their race medal and shirt the next day. They might as well wear a sign on their back that says, "Yes, I did just voluntarily kick my butt yesterday, and you?" If you are like my friend, Tia, you may even wear your medal on your return flight home, as it just might help you with a seat upgrade! Earning all of the different race medals is part of the fun of racing. For most of the big marathons, a local running store or a vendor at the expo may even provide free, if not discounted, medal engraving. If you are like me and want to save your money for race entries, just use a permanent marker and write your race time on the back of the medal. Once your medal collection grows, there are companies that make medal hangers so that you can display them on your wall. Before I started donating my medals to Medals4Mettle.org, I would use a 20-prong tie rack to display my medals. Granted, I had four tie racks holding up my 85 medals. I also framed some of my favorite race posters. The medals and the posters made up my inspiration room.

Marathon in Review

I know it might be too early to think about Marathoning 102 but just in case, I recommend that you write a quick race recap for yourself. This will help you for your next marathon. You can even log this information on the back of your race bib. To help other runners that may run the same marathon, you could even add a race review to bibzz.net and raceraves. com

Here are some questions to help with your marathon recap:

- What worked race eve, pre-race, during the race and after the race?

- What didn't work race eve, pre-race, during the race and after the race?

- What kind of pacing did you follow during the race? Would you change this for your next marathon?

- When did you take in nutrition? What and how much nutrition did you take in?

- Did you use any of the course nutrition and hydration?

- What were the weather conditions pre-race and during the race?

- What gear did you run in from head to toe? Would you have done anything different gear wise?

- At what mile do you hit your wall? Was the wall mental, physical or both? What could you do differently to prolong this from happening in your next marathon?

AID STATION 1— TRAINING PLANS

As mentioned in Mile 4, before starting any fitness regimen, I recommend that you first see your doctor to obtain medical clearance. For marathon training, I also recommend that you have a strong running base in which you can comfortably run a 4 to 6-mile long run and comfortably average 15 to 20 miles a week. Having this base fitness will provide a strong foundation to start building your mileage up to the big kahuna; 26.2! Once you have these prerequisites checked off, you can choose your syllabus below! One way to get to this base fitness is to find a 10K race that is about a month from when you need to kick off your marathon training. Train and then race for that 10K and BOOM, you will be ready for my class. Although it is not necessary, if you want to have an even strong running base, you can train and race a half-marathon that is 4 to 6 weeks before your marathon kick off.

Depending upon your current running fitness level, I have provided two unique training plans to choose from. Each plan has been designed to allow for proper buildup of mileage week to week and also proper recovery between training runs.

It's a good idea to sign up for at least one race during your marathon training season. Ideally a half-marathon but even a 5K will give you practice with packet pick up, race day pacing, gear check, corral cut-offs, aid station navigation, timing and content of nutrition, "chafing management" and even your "plumbing management", so to speak.

Try not to get overwhelmed as the mileage builds up to the 20-22-mile-long run. In running and in life, focus on one step at a time and you will get there.

Workout Key:

Cross Training—As referenced in Mile 9, cross training and strength training has been incorporated into each training plan as a way to help minimize injuries. On your cross-training days, you want to make sure that you are not doing anything high impact on your lower body. For example, pilates, yoga, swimming, walking rowing are great cross training options because they have minimal weight-bearing impact on our legs.

Rest Days - Rest days are just as important as training days because they allow your muscles, bones and connective tissue time to rebuild from the wear and tear created from each run. Having your eye on the prize for 20 weeks can also take a toll on your psyche. That is why rest days also give us a mental break from the intensity of the training

Long Run - The long runs are the most important run of the week because they mimic race day the most. Each week they allow you to fine tune what will work and not work on race day in regards to nutrition, pacing and gear. I recommend with your long runs that you focus on completing the mileage and also running the second half faster than the first half: negative splitting.

AWESOME Plan - This plan is recommended if you are new to running or if you are just getting back into running.

WEEK	MON	TUES	WED	THURS	FRI	SAT	SUN	TOTAL
1	Easy 3.0	Cross Train or Rest	Easy 3.0	Easy 3.0	Rest	Long 5.0	Cross Train or Rest	14.0
2	Easy 4.0	Cross Train or Rest	Easy 4.0	Easy 3.0	Rest	Long 6.0	Cross Train or Rest	17.0
3	Easy 5.0	Cross Train or Rest	Easy 4.0	Easy 3.0	Rest	Long 7.0	Cross Train or Rest	19.0
4	Easy 5.0	Cross Train or Rest	Easy 4.0	Easy 4.0	Rest	Long 8.0	Cross Train or Rest	21.0
5	Easy 5.0	Cross Train or Rest	Easy 4.5	Easy 4.0	Rest	Long 6.0	Cross Train or Rest	19.5
6	Easy 5.0	Cross Train or Rest	Easy 4.5	Easy 4.0	Rest	Long 9.0	Cross Train or Rest	22.5
7	Easy 6.0	Cross Train or Rest	Easy 5.0	Easy 5.0	Rest	Long 10.0	Cross Train or Rest	26.0
8	Easy 6.0	Cross Train or Rest	Easy 5.0	Easy 5.0	Rest	Long 12.0	Cross Train or Rest	28.0
9	Easy 6.0	Cross Train or Rest	Easy 5.0	Easy 5.0	Rest	Long 8.0	Cross Train or Rest	24.0
10	Easy 6.0	Cross Train or Rest	Easy 5.0	Easy 5.0	Rest	Long 13.0	Cross Train or Rest	29.0
11	Easy 7.0	Cross Train or Rest	Easy 6.0	Easy 6.0	Rest	Long 15.0	Cross Train or Rest	34.0

12	Easy 7.0	Cross Train or Rest	Easy 6.0	Easy 6.0	Rest	Long 16.0	Cross Train or Rest	35.0
13	Easy 7.0	Cross Train or Rest	Easy 6.0	Easy 6.0	Rest	Long 12.0	Cross Train or Rest	31.0
14	Easy 7.0	Cross Train or Rest	Easy 6.0	Easy 6.0	Rest	Long 17.0	Cross Train or Rest	36.0
15	Easy 7.0	Cross Train or Rest	Easy 6.0	Easy 6.0	Rest	Long 18.0	Cross Train or Rest	37.0
16	Easy 8.0	Cross Train or Rest	Easy 7.0	Easy 6.0	Rest	Long 12.0	Cross Train or Rest	33.0
17	Easy 8.0	Cross Train or Rest	Easy 6.0	Easy 6.0	Rest	Long 20.0	Cross Train or Rest	40.0
18	Easy 6.0	Cross Train or Rest	Easy 5.0	Easy 4.0	Rest	Long 8.0	Cross Train or Rest	23.0
19	Easy 6.0	Cross Train or Rest	Easy 4.0	Easy 4.0	Rest	Long 8.0	Cross Train or Rest	22.0
20	Easy 4.0	Cross Train or Rest	Easy 4.0	Easy 4.0	Rest	Easy 2.62 Shakeout Run	10 Minute Easy 26.2 Baby!	40.82

BRAVO PLAN -This plan is recommended if you have recently run a half-marathon and or if you have been running consistently for a year or more.

WEEK	MON	TUES	WED	THURS	FRI	SAT	SUN	TOTAL
1	Easy 5.0	Cross Train or Rest	Easy 4.0	Easy 5.0	Rest	Long 7.0	Easy 3.0	24.0
2	Easy 5.0	Cross Train or Rest	Easy 4.0	Easy 5.0	Rest	Long 8.0	Easy 3.0	25.0
3	Easy 5.0	Cross Train or Rest	Easy 4.0	Easy 5.0	Rest	Long 9.0	Easy 3.0	26.0
4	Easy 6.0	Cross Train or Rest	Easy 5.0	Easy 5.0	Rest	Long 10.0	Easy 4.0	30.0
5	Easy 6.0	Cross Train or Rest	Easy 5.5	Easy 5.0	Rest	Long 8.0	Easy 4.0	28.5
6	Easy 6.0	Cross Train or Rest	Easy 6.0	Easy 6.0	Rest	Long 11.0	Easy 4.0	33.0
7	Easy 6.0	Cross Train or Rest	Easy 6.0	Easy 7.0	Rest	Long 12.0	Easy 5.0	36.0
8	Easy 7.0	Cross Train or Rest	Easy 6.0	Easy 7.0	Rest	Long 13.0	Easy 5.0	38.0
9	Easy 7.0	Cross Train or Rest	Easy 6.5	Easy 7.0	Rest	Long 11.0	Easy 5.0	36.5
10	Easy 7.0	Cross Train or Rest	Easy 6.5	Easy 7.0	Rest	Long 15.0	Easy 6.0	41.5

11	Easy 7.0	Cross Train or Rest	Easy 6.5	Easy 8.0	Rest	Long 16.0	Easy 6.0	43.5
12	Easy 7.0	Cross Train or Rest	Easy 7.0	Easy 8.0	Rest	Long 17.0	Easy 6.0	45.0
13	Easy 8.0	Cross Train or Rest	Easy 7.0	Easy 8.0	Rest	Long 18.0	Easy 6.0	47.0
14	Easy 8.0	Cross Train or Rest	Easy 7.0	Easy 8.0	Rest	Long 10.0	Easy 7.0	40.0
15	Easy 8.0	Cross Train or Rest	Easy 7.0	Easy 8.0	Rest	Long 20.0	Easy 3.0	46.0
16	Easy 8.0	Cross Train or Rest	Easy 7.0	Easy 7.0	Rest	Long 10.0	Easy 7.0	39.0
17	Easy 7.0	Cross Train or Rest	Easy 6.0	Easy 7.0	Rest	Long 22.0	Easy 3.0	45.0
18	Easy 6.0	Cross Train or Rest	Easy 6.0	Easy 6.0	Rest	Long 10.0	Rest	28.0
19	Easy 6.0	Cross Train or Rest	Easy 5.0	Easy 6.0	Rest	Long 8.0	Rest	25.0
20	Easy 5.0	Cross Train or Rest	Easy 5.0	Easy 5.0	Rest	Easy 2.62 Shakeout Run	10 Minute Easy 26.2 Baby!	43.82

AID STATION 2—DYNAMIC AND STATIC STRETCHES

As discussed in Mile 16, stretching before and after your run will help minimize injury. The following illustrations have been provided by my pre-hab and re-hab expert, Dr. Mark W. Baker, D.C. of Elite Healthcare in Chicago.

Dynamic Stretches - It is recommended that you do these stretches *before* your run. Repeat each dynamic stretch 5 to 10 times for each side of your body.

Forward/ Reverse Lunge

Starting from a standing position step out with one foot to a comfortable distance while keeping your posture erect and your trailing leg slightly bent. Bend the front knee to approximately a 90° angle but try not to allow your knee to go past your toes. Push yourself back up to the starting position. This stretches the trailing leg hip flexors and increases mobility to the hips and ankles.

Repeat on opposite side.

Perform 5-10 repetitions per side.

* To perform a reverse lunge, just maintain the same posture, but step back with one leg.

Single Leg Hip Hinge

Stand with your feet shoulder-width apart. Lift one foot off the ground, keeping a very soft bend in the grounded knee and hinge from your hips while reaching forward and stretching the grounded hamstring. Return to starting position. To increase the effectiveness of this stretch, try to hold for a 3 second count at the end of your reach and try to keep the lifted leg from touching the ground for balance between repetitions. Remember to keep the low back neutral during this movement and make sure not to flex forward from the lumbar spine. This dynamic warm up is great for stretching the hamstrings, helping your balance, and strengthening the muscles in the grounded leg.

Repeat on opposite side.

Perform 5-10 repetitions per side.

Lateral Lunge

Standing straight up, step out to your side with one foot. Place your arms in front of you for counterbalance. Keeping the trailing leg straight, bend the forward leg until you feel tension in the trailing leg. Return to starting position. In each subsequent attempt, try to go slightly deeper.

This stretches almost all of the muscles in your lower body (quadriceps gluteus maximus, adductor muscles along your inner thighs, etc.)

Repeat on opposite side.

Perform 5-10 repetitions per side.

Static Stretches -Static stretches are most effective when performed after your workout. Try to hold each stretch for a minimum of 30 seconds.

Bent Leg Calf Stretch

Stand facing a wall with your arms straight in front of you pressing into the wall. Keep one foot forward and the back foot with the heel flat on the ground. Bend the back knee straight as you lean toward the wall. The further back the trailing leg, the quicker you will feel this stretch. Stretch until you feel a deep stretch in the back calf. Hold for about 30 seconds then switch legs.

This stretch is primarily a stretch for the soleus (calf muscle).

Repeat on the opposite side.

Repeat 3-5 times.

Straight Leg Calf Stretch

Stand facing a wall with your arms straight in front of you pressing into the wall. Keep one foot forward and the back foot with the heel flat on the ground. Keep the back knee straight as you lean toward the wall (the further back the trailing leg, the quicker you will feel this stretch) until you feel a deep stretch in the back calf. Hold for about 30 seconds then switch legs. This stretch is primarily a stretch for the gastrocnemius (calf muscle)

Repeat on the opposite side.

Repeat 3-5 times.

Hamstring Stretch

Start by sitting on the ground with your legs straight out in front of you. Try to straighten your knees and pull your toes back toward your head. Now, keeping your low back straight and hinging through your hips, bend as far forward as you can. If your hamstrings are very tight, you may only get to your ankles, but if your flexibility is better, you may get past your ankles. Hold that position for a minimum of 30 seconds.

Repeat 3-5 times.

Kneeling Hip Flexor Stretch

Start with a pad, pillow, mat, or something very soft about 6" from a wall. Place a knee on that object and place that same side foot up the wall. Place your other foot on the ground in front of you with that knee over the ankle. Keeping your posture erect, lean forward until you feel a deep stretch in the hip flexors on the side that is contacting the wall. This stretches the hip flexors and quadriceps.

Hold that stretch for a minimum of 30 seconds.

Repeat on the opposite side.

Repeat 3-5 times.

AID STATION 3—MARATHON CHECK LIST

Use the following checklist as a baseline to start your own race day check list:

Marathon Check List

Before/During Race

- [ ] Race Bib/Timing Chip/Race Belt
- [ ] Running Shoes
- [ ] Warm Up Clothes *(throw away)*
- [ ] Women: Sports Bra/Top/Bottom
- [ ] Men:Top/Bottom
- [ ] Socks/Compression Socks or Sleeves
- [ ] Nutrtion/Hydration
- [ ] Hydration Belt/Bottle
- [ ] Visor/Hat/Sunglasses
- [ ] Enable Do Not Disturb or Airplane Mode on Phone
- [ ] Gloves/Arm Warmers/Knit Hat/Hand Warmers
- [ ] Anti-Chafing Gel or Stick
- [ ] Sunscreen
- [ ] Watch/GPS/Heart Rate Monitor

Post Race

- [ ] Gear Check Bag
- [ ] Change of Clothes
- [ ] Compression Tights/Socks
- [ ] Change of Shoes/Flip Flops
- [ ] Recovery Nutrition/Hydration
- [ ] Baby Wipes/Towel
- [ ] Meet Up Spot for Family & Friends
- [ ] Phone Charger

AID STATION 4— ACKNOWLEDGEMENTS

This book would have stayed on my "someday list" if it weren't for one of my clients (client that turns into a friend) giving me homework. Even before I started coaching, the universe would bring first-time marathoners and future first-time marathoners into my day to day path. They would be rightfully SCITED and/or full of self-doubt. I would calm their nerves, share some of my Denise-isms and send them off more excited than scared about running a marathon. Before departing though, a lot of them would tell me, "You should write a book!" I would reply, "I will someday." That someday came in May 2015 when I met Joel Thomason. I had met Joel a month prior when we both were on the same bus heading to Hopkinton, Massachusetts. That bus was taking us to the start line of Boston. This was Joel's first Boston and he was a little anxious. After all, he was running THEE Boston. Nothing comes close to the feelings of your first marathon until you run the holy grail of marathoning, Boston. I shared some of my Denise-isms with Joel on our bus ride. Shortly after returning home, he reached out to me to coach him for his next marathon. We subsequently met for breakfast to talk about training options and all things marathoning. During this discussion, he also said, "You should write a book" and I said, "I will someday." That is when he made my talk, no longer cheap! Joel told me that he was going to do my homework (his training plan), but he also gave me homework! He told me to come up with three things that I would put in my book. He told me this homework had to be completed by our next one-on-one session. I went for a run later that week and thought about my homework. BOOM, I came up with the concept and title of Me, You and 26.2 just like that. Thank You, Joel! Thank you for believing in me until I believed it. I am turning in my last homework assignment to you now!

I also have to thank my editors and "no longer first-timers", Emily Lane (Mile 11) and Allie Maloney for keeping Me, You & 26.2 grounded in the trenches of a first-time marathoner's shoes and not a 100-time marathoner's shoes. You both were instrumental in fine tuning this book and keeping me on track. I could not have gotten to this finish line without you both.

Thank you to my mom, Judy and my dad, Tom, for always being there no matter what adventures and mis-adventures I brought myself to. You taught me grit, perseverance and that I should never lose the ability to laugh at myself.

Thank you to my siblings, Dawn, Debbie, Angie, Mike and my stepmom, Theresa for always supporting me in whatever I put my heart into.

Thank you to my soul sister, Hedy, for keeping me grounded when I get too high or too low.

Thank you to the team of doctors that put me back together and have kept me running since my re-birthday. This includes the Emergency Room staff at New York Presbyterian, Dr. Terry Nicola, Dr. Mark Baker and his team at Elite Healthcare and Dr Lisa Schoene.

Thank You to Jessica Migala for helping me jump start my book when I first reached out to you looking for direction back on July 7, 2015.

Thank you to Joey and his welcoming team at the Des Plaines and Kinzie Starbucks. You not only kept me highly caffeinated to translate my Denise-isms onto paper but you also allowed me to become a semi-permanent fixture vente after vente. Not to mention, you are the only Starbucks that got to know my name!

Lastly, thank you to all of my first-timer and many-timer runners who let this Energizer Runner into their world. You inspire me and fill my soul. You are my daily reminder that I so made the right decision on June 3rd, 2016!

ABOUT THE AUTHOR

Coach Denise Sauriol, a.k.a, Marathon Whisperer, ran her first marathon in 1994 and that finish line turned her "I can't" into "What else can I do?!" This soul-igniting, self-talk transformation is what she aims to share with non-runners and fellow runners alike. SCITED (Scared + Excited) like her first-timers, Denise most recently left her 26-year career in accounting to coach full-time. Her passion for coaching began in 2010 after she survived a near fatal car accident. She is a certified running coach through Road Runners Club of America and USA Track and Field. She has competed in over 100 marathons (including 11 Boston Marathons, 23 Chicago Marathons, a 100-mile ultra-marathon and two Ironman triathlons.) She is also a Co-founder of Girls on the Run-Chicago. Like most of her clients, she also had bad memories of running the one-mile time trial in gym class. Now that she is her own gym teacher, she has fun on every run! When she is not running the world, she lives in Chicago, Illinois with Farley (Labrador Retriever) and Stuey (Persian cat) her assistant coaches. Denise is also available for motivational speaking engagements for kids and adults.

Contact and follow Coach Denise on:

- Instagram: @meyouand262
- Twitter: @meyouand262
- Website and Blog: run-for-change.com

Courage Begets Courage